WARBIRD**TECH**
S E R I E S

VOLUME 31

BOEING
F/A-18 HORNET

BY BRAD ELWARD

specialtypress

PUBLISHERS AND WHOLESALERS

Front Cover: *Two VMFA-134 Hornets (MF 09 BuNo. 162455 and MF 03 BuNo. 162407) fly over California with bomb loads.* (Ted Carlson)

Back Cover (Left Top): *The Hornet's speed brake is located on the upper fuselage between the engines and vertical stabilizers. This photo was taken from the port side and shows the activator.* (Ted Carlson)

Back Cover (Right Top): *The Super Hornet will form the backbone of American naval aviation for the next 25 years. The Super Hornet can perform all tactical missions presently covered by the Hornet, Tomcat, and Prowler, and can serve as an organic tanker and reconnaissance platform.* (Boeing via Dennis R. Jenkins)

Back Cover (Lower): *A composite drawing of the F/A-18.* (Boeing via Dennis R. Jenkins)

Title Page: *The Super Hornet's engine intakes and wheel-well doors are especially designed to reduce radar cross section. Eventually, two squadrons of F/A-18Es will deploy on each carrier, with one 14 plane squadron of F/A-18Fs and one F/A-18C squadron, although the latter will be replaced with JSF once it enters service.* (Boeing)

TABLE OF CONTENTS

BOEING F/A-18 HORNET AND SUPER HORNET

PREFACE

During the summer of 2000, a series of events occurred that might not seem significant to the average American. To the defense community, and to those in naval aviation in particular, these events highlight the tremendous impact on naval aviation of one of the most important weapons platforms of the latter part of the 20th Century: the Boeing F/A-18 Hornet. In June, VFA-122, the Navy's F/A-18E/F Fleet Readiness Squadron (FRS) at NAS Lemoore, began training aircrews for the new Super Hornet, with plans for the aircraft's first deployment by VFA-115 in 2002 aboard USS *Abraham Lincoln* (CVN-72). Another historical milestone occurred on 25 August: the close of the F/A-18 Hornet line, with the last two-place "D" model leaving Boeing for its new home with VMFA(AW)-121 stationed at MCAS Miramar, California. Perhaps the most significant of all these events occurred at 1200 hours EST on 14 September when the combined Hornet community surpassed the 4,000,000th flight hour mark.

This latter event reflects the Hornet's heavy usage during the 1990s as well as the fact that 55 active-duty and reserve Navy and Marine Corps squadrons currently operate the Hornet, with two-to-three squadrons deploying on every U.S. Navy carrier at sea. Moreover, Hornets are flown by air forces of seven foreign countries, and are the aircraft of choice of the U.S. Navy's Flight Demonstration Team, the *Blue Angels*. Indeed, the pace of operations has been so hectic that some

300 older Hornets are in danger of surpassing their projected fatigue life and may be forced to undergo a service life extension program.

While many have criticized certain aspects of the Hornet throughout its twenty-some year life, few can dispute that it has now assumed center stage as the preeminent strike-fighter platform in the world. At the beginning of a new millennium, the Hornet stands in a position that few aircraft have stood in before. The F/A-18C serves as the backbone of the U.S. Navy carrier air wings, flying fighter and strike missions; the two-place F/A-18D provides the Marines with an all-weather, day/night fighter, attack, and reconnaissance platform; and the new F/A-18E/F Super Hornet is entering the fleet in 2001, bringing with it the capability to fulfill all tactical missions (plus organic tanking and reconnaissance), and potentially the electronic warfare mission now handled by the EA-6B Prowler. Without question, the Super Hornet will form the backbone of naval aviation well into the 2020s and will be sent into harm's way when that infamous question is asked, "Where are the carriers?"

The Hornet has come a long way from its origins as the Northrop YF-17 prototype in the Air Force's Light Weight Fighter (LWF) competition during the early 1970s. Although the General Dynamics YF-16 was selected by the Air Force, the Northrop product (when teamed with McDonnell Douglas) proved the most adaptable for carrier operations, and became the F-18

and A-18 Hornet. Through numerous technological breakthroughs in radar and cockpit design that gave one pilot the means to perform two separate and distinct missions, the F/A-18 multi-mission strike-fighter was borne, giving the Navy and Marines one aircraft capable of performing a wide spectrum of missions.

When it entered service in 1983, the F/A-18A proved to be an agile fighter and a proficient day bomber, but lacked true night and all-weather capabilities. The F/A-18B, while retaining a basic combat capability, served primarily as a trainer, although some were later used by VAQ-34's electronic warfare aggressors. In the late 1980s, the C and D models emerged, with a much-improved avionics package that expanded the aircraft's capabilities many-fold. These were followed in 1989 by the Night Attack configured C/D models, which today form all but a few Navy/Marine Corps strike-fighter squadrons, and which are uniquely responsible for bringing the night back to naval aviation as the Grumman A-6E Intruder retired. As the 1990s began, it became apparent that the growth potential of the C/D was virtually used up. This limitation, and the desire to enhance payload, survivability, as well as bring-back carriage, led to the F/A-18E/F Super Hornet, which was approved for Low Rate Initial Production on 28 March 1996 and has just recently been granted approval to issue a 5-year, 222 aircraft production contract and a planned production run of at least 548 aircraft.

Hornets can carry virtually all weaponry in the Navy/Marine Corps arsenal. Moreover, Hornets routinely post the highest mission-capable rates, boarding rates, and serve as the least maintenance-intensive aircraft fleetwide. Although the Super Hornet has yet to hit the fleet, it has already proven itself to be a winner. Indeed, if the Super Hornet evolves as significantly as did the F/A-18A, it will unquestionably go down in naval aviation annals as one of the most incredible naval aircraft ever built.

Brad Elward
May 2001

ACKNOWLEDGMENTS

Special thanks to Ellen LeMond-Holman (Manager, U.S. Navy and Marine Corps Programs, Boeing) and Denise Deon (F/A-18 Public Affairs) for their gracious and never-ending assistance. Thanks to Ned Conger; Dennis R. Jenkins; Laurie Tall (CHINFO); VADM Joseph Dyer, USN (currently Commander, Naval Air Systems Command, and formerly F/A-18 Program Manager, 1994-97); RADM James B. Godwin, III, USN (currently Program Executive Officer for Tactical Aircraft Programs and formerly F/A-18 Program Manager, 1997-2000); CAPT Jeff Wieringa (current F/A-18 Program Manager, 2000-); CAPT Robert H. Rutherford, USN (CO, VX-9 during F/A-18E/F OPEVAL); CDR Dave Dunaway, USN (current F/A-18 Radar IPT Lead AESA Program Manager and former EMD & VX-9 OpEval pilot); Bill Stussie (current Deputy Assistant Secretary of the Navy (RD&A) and former F/A-18 Deputy Program Manager during the E/F development); RADM George Strohsahl, USN (F/A-18 Program Manager, 1983-1986); CAPT Scott Swift, USN (CO, VFA-122); CDR Robert F. Wood, USN (Ret);and VFA-106; Lon Nordeen, Manager, Business Development, Boeing; James Sandberg, Northrop-Grumman. Thanks also goes to Barb Joyner, who provided valuable research for this project and helped with the preparation of many of the diagrams and appendices. Hopefully, the inaccuracies have been kept to a minimum; those that remain are my own. All technical information concerning performance has come from open public sources.

Much of the photography in this work can be credited to Ted Carlson, one of the world's leading aviation photographers. Photographs were also generously supplied by Mark Munzel; Don Linn; John Binford; Robert F. Dorr; Darryl Shaw; LCDR Richard Burgess, USN (Ret); LCDR Richard Morgan, USN (Ret); Hill Goodspeed (National Naval Museum of Aviation); Larry Merritt (Boeing); and the U.S. Navy.

I sincerely thank my wife Marie for all her support and patience throughout this project as I strived to meet my deadlines and to prepare a thorough representation of this great aircraft.

The two-seat F/A-18F was used for carrier qualifications; during the F/A-18A/B EMD phase, the single-seat A-model was used, in part to quell fears in the F-14 and A-6 communities that the Hornet might replace them. A close-up of this F/A-18F highlights the drooped main gear and extended nose gear. (Boeing)

A fully-loaded F/A-18 with two AIM-7 Sparrows (on the fuselage), two AIM-9 Sidewinders (wingtips), and two AGM-88 HARMs, plus three 330-gallon fuel tanks. (U.S. Navy)

This VFA-15 F/A-18A (BuNo. 163126) was photographed aboard the USS Theodore Roosevelt *(CVN-71) during Operation Desert Storm in January 1991.* (Rick Morgan)

ORIGINS OF THE HORNET

1

THE LIGHTWEIGHT FIGHTER COMPETITION

The Boeing F/A-18 Hornet traces its roots back to an Air Force effort to develop a light-weight fighter as a complement to the complex and expensive F-15 Eagle air superiority fighter. During the mid-1960s, the principal Air Force interceptor/fighter was the McDonnell Douglas F-4 Phantom II. Introduced in 1961, the Phantom quickly became the front-line fighter for all three services and was soon adapted to the air-to-ground role as well. However, as Vietnam air engagements soon proved, the larger F-4 was difficult to fight against the smaller, more nimble MiGs. There was still a need for an improved fighter with a look-down mode radar and missile system and enhanced maneuverability.

In April 1965, the Air Force initiated a study to develop a new dedicated air superiority fighter, designated Fighter, Experimental or FX, which would later evolve into the F-15. Later that year, the Air Force's Tactical Air Command (TAC) released Qualitative Operations Requirement (QOR) 65-14-F setting forth the need for a new air superiority fighter, with a high thrust-to-weight ratio, an advanced air-to-air radar, and speed in excess of Mach 2.5. The aircraft was also to utilize the latest in short-range and beyond-visual-range (BVR) air-to-air missiles. On 5 November 1965, the FX became the official effort to replace the F-4, and by early December, a request for proposals was released containing the aircraft's initial parameters.

Although the light-weight fighter

(LWF) design was first conceived during the mid-1960s, because of fears that a smaller aircraft necessarily meant one less capable, no real consideration was given to the concept. However, with the rising costs of the FX program, and a growing perception that the Soviet Union was numerically eliminating the U.S. technical advantage, the time seemed right during the early 1970s to revisit the LWF as complement, rather than as an alternative, to the FX program.

Therefore, on 24 August 1971, the Air Force announced plans for a fly-off to evaluate two yet-to-be submitted LWF prototypes. As a side note, and quite prophetic of things to come, the Navy was instructed by Congress to monitor the LWF program and determine whether either of the

competitors could be made suitable for carrier operations. Following months of discussions in Congress, $12 million (from Fiscal Year 1972) was appropriated for the program on 14 December 1971. Program implementation plans were quickly devised and approved and on 31 December, the Request for Proposal (RFP) and model contract to the industry were released, marking the official start of the LWF program.

Less than a week later, the 21-page LWF RFP outlining the performance and cost goals was presented to nine companies, Northrop and General Dynamics among them. Generally, the RFP called for a highly-maneuverable, high thrust-to-weight fighter, with simple avionics and a basic fire-control system. The airframe had to withstand a 6.5-g

The McDonnell F-4 Phantom II was the workhorse of the Vietnam War, seeing action in all three services as a fighter, bomber, and reconnaissance platform. The F-4, however, was not an agile fighter and only those flown by Navy air crews faired well against the MiGs of the Vietnamese People's Air Force (VPAF). (National Naval Aviation Museum)

Designed as an air superiority fighter from the start, the McDonnell Douglas F-15 Eagle, formerly known as the F-X program, has become the standard by which air superiority aircraft are measured. Due to its cost and complexity, Air Force planners soon realized that they could not procure the F-15 in adequate numbers to meet the perceived threat and thus, the Light Weight Fighter (LWF) concept was born. (Ted Carlson)

The Navy had its own large, expensive fighter to match the F-15, the Grumman F-14 Tomcat. Key to the Tomcat was its sophisticated radar and weapons suite, which included the AIM-54 Phoenix. The navalized YF-17 was intended to complement the Tomcat, by serving as a light fighter and a light attack aircraft to replace the F-4, A-4 Skyhawk, and A-7 Corsair II. These two F-14As are from VF-213. (Ted Carlson)

load, with a gross weight not to exceed 20,000 lbs. The RFP placed a limit of $3 million per copy based upon a buy of 300 planes over a three-year production contract.

On 18 February, five of the companies submitted proposals: Lockheed, Northrop, Boeing, Ling Timco Vought (LTV), and General Dynamics. These proposals were reviewed over the next few weeks and in mid-March the results were announced with Boeing's Model 908-909, General Dynamics' Model 401-16B, and Northrop's Model P-600, all making the final cut; Lockheed's and LTV's proposals were rejected. After further analysis, the General Dynamics Model was selected as the most desirable, followed by the Northrop design. Boeing's offer fell to third, as it was too similar to that of General Dynamics and it was desired that the two prototypes represent divergent approaches to the LWF design. Boeing's design was similar in looks and performance to that submitted by General Dynamics, but more expensive. On 13 April, the General Dynamics and the Northrop submissions were selected for the fly-off.

That decision resulted in a $37,943,000 contract for two General Dynamics Model 401-16Bs (YF-16 Nos. 72-1567 and -1568) and one for $39,878,715 for two Northrop Model P-600s (YF-17 Nos. 72-1569 and -1570). Each contract provided enough funding for the design and construction of two prototypes, plus 300 hours of flight testing. A contract was also awarded to General Electric for further development of its YJ101-series engine, and to Pratt & Whitney for continued work on the F100 engine. The fly-off competition was to commence as soon as the two prototypes had demonstrated their initial flight-worthiness.

Need Emerges in the Navy

While the Navy had been watching the development of the LWF program, it had been busy with its own agenda. The Navy had developed its own air superiority fighter (under the VF-X program), the Grumman F-14 Tomcat. Like the Eagle, the Tomcat represented the "high-end" of the fighter spectrum, both in cost and performance. The Navy soon realized that it too needed a low-cost companion for the sophisticated Tomcat, but one that could also replace the aging A-4 Skyhawk, A-7, and F-4 in the light-attack role.

During the summer of 1973, the Navy was ordered to pursue a low-cost alternative to continued production of the F-14, as its costs were now exceeding high, and in Sep-tember of that year, the Navy issued a formal request for proposals. The Navy was now seeking combined air-to-air and air-to-ground plat-form, which was termed VFA-X for Naval Fighter-Attack, Experimental. At about that same time, a debate was raging within the Navy, similar to that within the Air Force, as to the propriety of an LWF and the so-called "hi-lo mix". Opponents of the LWF requirement maintained that there was still a basic requirement for a BVR missile capability. This meant a larger radar, and hence a larger overall design, which ran con-trary to the LWF concept. Indeed, one group even offered a stripped-down version of the F-14 (without its Phoenix missile system, but retaining the AIM-7 capability), known as the F-14X. This was soon rejected. The Navy also experiment-ed with the idea of a navalized ver-sion of the F-15, but it proved far too costly and the heavier gear led to added weight.

The Navy Shifts Gears

On 10 May 1974 Congress nixed the VFA-X program and its $34 million funding request, and ordered the Navy to consider adopting one of the two LWF prototypes then under-going testing by the Air Force. Although the Senate had approved the funding, the House Appropria-tions Committee wanted to termi-nate the program all together. What resulted was a compromise, with a new program called the Naval Air Combat Fighter (NACF) substituted in place of VFA-X.

The managers are in agreement on

NORTHROP LIGHTWEIGHT FIGHTER EVOLUTION					LWF PROPOSAL	CARRIER-BASED F-18A
					P610 TWIN ENGINE LWF	
HIGH-WING FORWARD INLETS	LARGER LERX INLETS UNDER LERX	TWIN VERTICAL STABILIZERS LARGER LERX	CONTOURED LERX EXTENSION LARGER VERTICAL STABILIZERS	REFINED FUSELAGE SHORTER INLETS	P600 SINGLE ENGINE LWF	YF-17 PROTOTYPE LAND-BASED F-18L
N-300	P530	P530-1	P530-2	P530-3	P6x0	
1966	1967	1968	1969	1970	1971-72	1973 1976

The N-300 marked the beginning of what we know today as the F-18. Began in 1965 as a Northrop project, the aircraft evolved into the P530 Cobra multi-mission aircraft and was later modified into a single-mission fighter to compete in the LWF competition. This modification produced the YF-17. (Northrop via Dennis R. Jenkins)

the appropriation of $20 million as proposed by the Senate instead of no funding as proposed by the House for the VFAX aircraft. The conferees support the need for a lower cost alternative fighter to complement the F-14A and replace F-4 and A-7 aircraft; however, the conferees direct that the development of this aircraft make maximum use of the air force lightweight fighter and Air Combat Fighter technology and hardware. The $20 million provided is to be placed in a new program titled "Navy Air Combat Fighter" rather than VFAX. Adaptation of the selected air force air combat fighter to be capable of carrier operations is the prerequisite for use of the funds provided. Funds may be released to a contractor for the purpose of designing the modifications required for navy use. Future funding is to be contingent upon the capability of the navy to produce a derivative of the air force air combat fighter design. (Kelly, Orr. *Hornet: The Inside Story of the F/A-18,* Presidio Press, 1990, pp. 14-15.)

Unlike its Air Force counterpart, however, the NACF would be capable of air-to-air and air-to-ground missions.

The Navy was understandably upset, recalling its ill-fated experience with the last aircraft the bureaucrats tried to force on both services: the F-111B. However, in accordance with the Congressional directive, naval aviators began working with the ACF team and evaluating both competitors for possible carrier usage. In late September 1974, the two manufacturers, both recognizing that they lacked any experience with carrier-based aircraft, sought affiliation with other aerospace companies which had already produced jets for the Navy. General Dynamics teamed up with LTV, which had produced the highly-successful F-8 Crusader and the A-7 Corsair II. Northrop teamed with McDonnell Douglas, the aerospace giant which had produced the A-3 Skywarrior and A-4 Skyhawk (as Douglas), and the F-4 Phantom II

and a host of earlier naval fighters (as McDonnell).

THE YF-16 DEMONSTRATOR

Built at the General Dynamics facility in Forth Worth, Texas, the YF-16 represented a leap in technology by way of its analog fly-by-wire (FBW) flight control system. With a wingspan of roughly 30'-0" and measuring just 46'-6", the YF-16 was small, and maneuverable. It featured one Pratt & Whitney F100-PE-100 23,500 lb.-thrust engine, a derivative of that used by the F-15, and could carry an external load of 13,200 lbs. With afterburner, the YF-16 was projected to have a 1.28:1 combat thrust-to-weight ratio. In addition to its evolutionary flight control system, it also featured another unique characteristic: the pilot sat reclined and used a side-stick controller, rather than the conventional center stick between the legs. The cockpit was also positioned higher, giving the pilot tremendous all-around visibility. The first YF-16 flew on 2 February 1974, and the second flew on 9 May. With basic tests now done, the YF-16 was ready to begin the LWF evaluation.

THE YF-17 DEMONSTRATOR

Northrop's proposal must truly be reviewed from a historical perspective. Its submission, the Model P600 (which became the YF-17), traces back to efforts by Northrop engineer Lee Begin to develop a light-weight fighter capable of high maneuverability and high angles-of-attack. Begin drew on the already successful F-5/T-38 family designs the company had made during the 1950s and early 1960s, as well as its earlier single-engine, delta-winged N-102 Fang. In 1965, Northrop began the N-300 program, which was essentially an F-5 with a stretched fuselage, two

One of the aircraft the Hornet replaced was the A-7 Corsair II. This capable aircraft served well during the Vietnam War and filled the light attack role into the early 1990s. (Ted Carlson)

engines, and the addition of small leading-edge root extensions, called LERXs, which created a vortex over the upper wing surfaces. These vortices served to separate the boundary layer air and improved maneuverability at high angles-of-attack.

The N-300 was originally powered by two 9,000-lb. thrust General Electric GE15-J1A1 turbojet engines, although these were later replaced by the more powerful GE15-J1A2. The final powerplant configuration saw use of the 13,000-lb. thrust J1A5 engines. Long oval-shaped inlet ducts, positioned far forward on the fuselage, fed air into the engines. These inlets were later positioned further back, and subse-

This Arizona Air National Guard F-16A represents the production version of the LWF competition winner. (Ted Carlson)

The aircraft's full-span leading-edge flaps are seen on this YF-17. The slots in the leading-edge root extension (LERX) that run along the side of the cockpit were included to prevent a build up of air ahead of the inlet during supersonic speeds. The slots also provided an escape for boundary-layer air during low-speed operations, but would later be filled almost entirely to reduce drag. The LERX added about 50 percent additional lift to the basic wings. (Northrop via Rick Burgess)

quently contoured into a canted "D" shape, with rounded edges. A splitter plate was also used between the engines and the fuselage to prevent boundary layer air from reaching the engines. In 1966, and after extensive wind tunnel testing, the wings were reconfigured at a higher position on the fuselage to optimize ordinance flexibility. Overall, the trapezoidal wing design was similar to the F-5s, with a quarter-chord line sweep of 20 degrees and an unswept trailing edge. Use was also made of full span leading- and half span trailing-edge flaps, and conventional ailerons. These flaps could be canted to increase lift at low speeds and during maneuvers. As the program progressed over the years, the wings migrated down to a mid-fuselage position, where they remained in the P530 and YF-17 prototype.

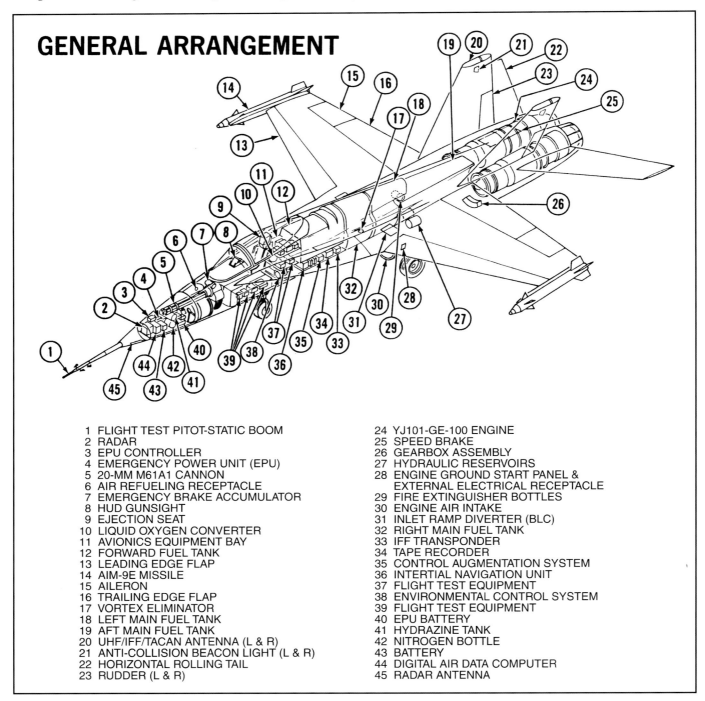

GENERAL ARRANGEMENT

1 FLIGHT TEST PITOT-STATIC BOOM	24 YJ101-GE-100 ENGINE
2 RADAR	25 SPEED BRAKE
3 EPU CONTROLLER	26 GEARBOX ASSEMBLY
4 EMERGENCY POWER UNIT (EPU)	27 HYDRAULIC RESERVOIRS
5 20-MM M61A1 CANNON	28 ENGINE GROUND START PANEL &
6 AIR REFUELING RECEPTACLE	EXTERNAL ELECTRICAL RECEPTACLE
7 EMERGENCY BRAKE ACCUMULATOR	29 FIRE EXTINGUISHER BOTTLES
8 HUD GUNSIGHT	30 ENGINE AIR INTAKE
9 EJECTION SEAT	31 INLET RAMP DIVERTER (BLC)
10 LIQUID OXYGEN CONVERTER	32 RIGHT MAIN FUEL TANK
11 AVIONICS EQUIPMENT BAY	33 IFF TRANSPONDER
12 FORWARD FUEL TANK	34 TAPE RECORDER
13 LEADING EDGE FLAP	35 CONTROL AUGMENTATION SYSTEM
14 AIM-9E MISSILE	36 INTERTIAL NAVIGATION UNIT
15 AILERON	37 FLIGHT TEST EQUIPMENT
16 TRAILING EDGE FLAP	38 ENVIRONMENTAL CONTROL SYSTEM
17 VORTEX ELIMINATOR	39 FLIGHT TEST EQUIPMENT
18 LEFT MAIN FUEL TANK	40 EPU BATTERY
19 AFT MAIN FUEL TANK	41 HYDRAZINE TANK
20 UHF/IFF/TACAN ANTENNA (L & R)	42 NITROGEN BOTTLE
21 ANTI-COLLISION BEACON LIGHT (L & R)	43 BATTERY
22 HORIZONTAL ROLLING TAIL	44 DIGITAL AIR DATA COMPUTER
23 RUDDER (L & R)	45 RADAR ANTENNA

The YF-17's general arrangement. (Northrop via Dennis R. Jenkins)

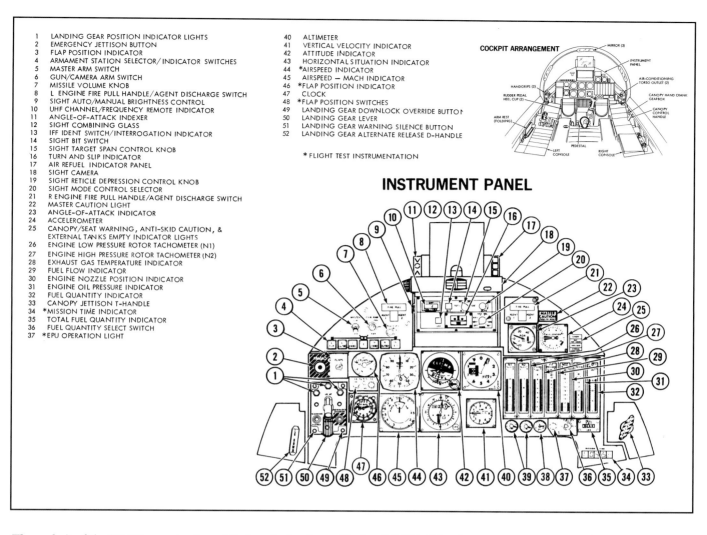

1   LANDING GEAR POSITION INDICATOR LIGHTS
2   EMERGENCY JETTISON BUTTON
3   FLAP POSITION INDICATOR
4   ARMAMENT STATION SELECTOR/ INDICATOR SWITCHES
5   MASTER ARM SWITCH
6   GUN/CAMERA ARM SWITCH
7   MISSILE VOLUME KNOB
8   L ENGINE FIRE PULL HANDLE/AGENT DISCHARGE SWITCH
9   SIGHT AUTO/MANUAL BRIGHTNESS CONTROL
10 UHF CHANNEL/FREQUENCY REMOTE INDICATOR
11 ANGLE-OF-ATTACK INDEXER
12 SIGHT COMBINING GLASS
13 IFF IDENT SWITCH/INTERROGATION INDICATOR
14 SIGHT BIT SWITCH
15 SIGHT TARGET SPAN CONTROL KNOB
16 TURN AND SLIP INDICATOR
17 AIR REFUEL INDICATOR PANEL
18 SIGHT CAMERA
19 SIGHT RETICLE DEPRESSION CONTROL KNOB
20 SIGHT MODE CONTROL SELECTOR
21 R ENGINE FIRE PULL HANDLE/AGENT DISCHARGE SWITCH
22 MASTER CAUTION LIGHT
23 ANGLE-OF-ATTACK INDICATOR
24 ACCELEROMETER
25 CANOPY/SEAT WARNING, ANTI-SKID CAUTION, &
    EXTERNAL TANKS EMPTY INDICATOR LIGHTS
26 ENGINE LOW PRESSURE ROTOR TACHOMETER (N1)
27 ENGINE HIGH PRESSURE ROTOR TACHOMETER (N2)
28 EXHAUST GAS TEMPERATURE INDICATOR
29 FUEL FLOW INDICATOR
30 ENGINE NOZZLE POSITION INDICATOR
31 ENGINE OIL PRESSURE INDICATOR
32 FUEL QUANTITY INDICATOR
33 CANOPY JETTISON T-HANDLE
34 *MISSION TIME INDICATOR
35 TOTAL FUEL QUANTITY INDICATOR
36 FUEL QUANTITY SELECT SWITCH
37 *EPU OPERATION LIGHT

40 ALTIMETER
41 VERTICAL VELOCITY INDICATOR
42 ATTITUDE INDICATOR
43 HORIZONTAL SITUATION INDICATOR
44 *AIRSPEED INDICATOR
45 AIRSPEED — MACH INDICATOR
46 *FLAP POSITION INDICATOR
47 CLOCK
48 *FLAP POSITION SWITCHES
49 LANDING GEAR DOWNLOCK OVERRIDE BUTTON
50 LANDING GEAR LEVER
51 LANDING GEAR WARNING SILENCE BUTTON
52 LANDING GEAR ALTERNATE RELEASE D-HANDLE

* FLIGHT TEST INSTRUMENTATION

COCKPIT ARRANGEMENT

INSTRUMENT PANEL

The cockpit of the YF-17 was simple, yet featured a heads-up display (HUD). (Northrop via Dennis R. Jenkins)

As the N-300 evolved into the P530 during 1967, the LERX was again enlarged. The engine inlets were moved even further under the LERX, although still not as far back as they are on the Hornet, and the design still retained the single vertical stabilizer of the F-5. It also featured all-moving stabilators mounted below midline. In 1968, however, the single vertical stabilizer was split into twin vertical stabilizers, each about one-half the size of the original vertical stabilizer, which canted outward at an almost 45-degree angle so that they would remain in the free-stream air flow. The single stabilizer was often blanketed in the wake of the wing during extreme angles-of-attacks. These stabilizers were doubled in size in 1969 and moved forward to a position partially overlapping the wings. The stabilizers were again enlarged during the following year, but the cant was reduced to 18 degrees. Yaw control was provided for by the placement of a rudder on each stabilizer, affixed low to minimize roll movement (cross-coupling) caused by the outwardly canting stabilizers.

What resulted was a near-Mach 2 aircraft with both an air-to-air and air-to-ground capability, and weighing approximately 40,000 lbs. Northrop first presented its P530 design, later called the Cobra, to the Air Force in early 1971, but quickly received a response of "lack of funds." Foreign interest was similarly weak when the aircraft was revealed at the January 1971 air show in Paris. When the Air Force announced the LWF competition, however, new life was breathed into the program. Northrop modified its Model P530, stripping it of its air-to-ground capability, and redesignated it as the Model P600. As part of the emphasis on air combat, the gun was moved from underneath the fuselage, where it was better suited to strafing, and placed in the nose, where it would work better in aerial combat. As a final modification, the YF-17 received the new General Electric 15,000-lb. thrust YJ101-GE-100 turbofan engines. These engines were mounted close together to minimize possible asymmetrical forces in the event of engine failure by one of the turbojets. Total weight was estimated at 23,000 pounds.

Principal features of the YF-17 included a Stencel Aero C ejection seat, a bubble canopy with superb aft visibility, a dorsally-mounted speed brake, and a Rockwell International ranging radar. The cockpit was well laid out and was equipped with a simple JLM International Head-up Display (HUD). The first YF-17 took to the skies at Edwards AFB on 9 June 1974 under the control of Northrop company test pilot Hank Chouteau, and the second YF-17 flew on 21 August.

LWF BECOMES THE ACF

Shortly after the LWF program was proposed, the Air Force announced that it was now "appropriate to consider full-scale development and eventual production of an ACF-type aircraft." Termed the Air Combat Fighter (ACF), the new program represented the Air Force's desire to adopt the previously rejected "hi-lo" mix of sophisticated, high-performance/high-cost fighters, and less expensive, good-performing aircraft. This "mix" would take advantage of the latest U.S. technology, yet provide enough planes to meet operational force commitments. In September, the Air Force announced that it would produce a minimum of 650 ACF, which had significant ramifications for the LWF (now ACF)

competition – the winner would receive a full production contract, and possibly huge foreign sales.

THE COMPETITION BEGINS

Although initially scheduled to last more than a year, the time table for the LWF/ACF competition was drastically shortened, and both contractors were instructed to complete their testing by mid-December 1974. The reason for this was simple: possible foreign sales. Several European countries were also interested in finding a new fighter to replace their fleets of F-104 and F-5 aircraft, which were now reaching the end of their service life. These countries – Belgium, Denmark, the Netherlands, and Norway – had formed a consortium called the Multinational Fighter Program Group (MFPG), and were considering the two U.S. LWF prototypes: the Dassault Mirage F.1 and the Saab JA-37 Viggen. Although the MFPG announced that it would look favorably at the winner of the Air Force LWF, the Group would make its decision in January 1975. Thus, there was tremendous incentive for the U.S. to complete the project and possibly capture the coveted foreign sales. Following the completion of its test company flights, the YF-16 quickly entered the fray.

The YF-17 flew a total of 288 test flights, accumulating some 345.5 flight hours, including 13 hours at supersonic flights. Interestingly, Northrop's second aircraft was late getting started, as the YJ101 engines were still undergoing tests and did not pass Preliminary Flight Rating Test (PFRT) until December 1973. This, in turn, significantly delayed the YF-17 program and delayed the aircraft's first flight. Thus, while

One of Northrop's goals was to secure a significant block of foreign sales. Here, ministers of defense from Belgium, Denmark, the Netherlands, and Norway gather to review the YF-17 prototype in September 1974. These same countries selected the YF-16 as their new fighter, following selection by the Air Force in January 1975. The loads are AGM-65 Mavericks, an AIM-7 Sparrow III, AIM-9 Sidewinders, and two Mk 80 series bombs. (Northrop via Rick Burgess)

Shown in its Air Force LWF competition markings, this YF-17 profile highlights the forward location of the stabilizers. The cockpit situation ensures excellent all-around visibility. (Northrop via Rick Burgess)

General Dynamics had two prototypes in the tests, only one YF-17 was available for flights until August. As a testament to its maintainability, the two YF-17s were still able to complete their missions, due in part to the Northrop teams' decision to fly the YF-17 on a demanding around-the-clock, three-shift schedule, seven days a week. Even so, this accelerated schedule did not permit Northrop to perform any modifications or to rectify any deficiencies discovered during the test program.

ACF evaluation flights were flown by military and civilian pilots, and most pilots were given several flights in each aircraft. Air-to-air engagements were flown under a variety of scenarios and against some of the leading "adversaries" of the day, including the F-4E, A-4, and the Convair F-106. Flights were also reportedly flown against some of the secretive "foreign" aircraft, the MiG-17, -21, and -23, operated by the Air Force. No flights were made against the F-14 or F-15, nor did the company prototypes ever fly against one another. The pilots noted that the YF-17 performed as advertised by Northrop, and rated it as satisfactory and a joy to fly. With a top speed of Mach 1.95 and a maximum altitude of approximately 50,000 feet, the YF-17 exhibited a peak load factor of 9.4 Gs and a sea-level rate of climb exceeding 50,000 feet per minute. Moreover, the aircraft was able to maintain a controllable angle-of-attack of 34 degrees in level flight and 63 degrees during a 60-degree zoom climb. Outstanding control was also demonstrated at air speeds as low as 20 knots.

On 13 January 1975, the results of the ACF program fly-off were finally announced – the winner was the General Dynamics YF-16. The reason for this selection was reportedly: the YF-16 presented slightly better performance (maneuverability, roll-rate, and range); it cost about $250,000 per unit less than the YF-17 as projected; and it offered commonality with the F-15's engine. The YF-17's engine, the J101, was still unproven and would require expensive logistics and technical support that the F100 would not, as it was just entering service with the F-15 fleet. The YF-16 was also, according to reports, a near unanimous choice of the competition pilots, who, incidentally, were predominantly Air Force.

LITTLE CHOICE FOR THE NAVY

The Navy was clearly disappointed with the outcome. Moreover, although General Dynamics had teamed up with a veteran Navy designer (Vought), the YF-16 proposal (called Model 1600) was proving difficult to convert to carrier operations. The Navy liked the YF-17's two-engine design, its apparent mission adaptability, and inherent room for growth. After months of discussions, an agreement was reached between the Navy and Congress and the Secretary of Defense and, on 2 May 1975, it was announced that the Navy would develop a derivative of the YF-17. A short time later, the aircraft was redesignated as the F-18 Naval Air Combat Fighter.

The eventual end-product of the LWF competition for the Navy was development of the F/A-18 from the YF-17. Here a Hornet from VFA-192 carries two AIM-9s, 4 Mk-82 500-lb. bombs, 1 AIM-7, and a centerline-mounted AAW-9 Walleye datalink pod. (CDR Tom Surbridge, USN via National Naval Aviation Museum)

The Navy demanded that the navalized YF-16 and YF-17 competitors be able to carry the AIM-7 beyond visual range (BVR) missile. This in turn required a larger radar than either competitor carried, necessitating a redesign of the forward fuselage/nose section. These ordnancemen are loading an AIM-7 on the fuselage station of a VFA-132 Privateer aboard USS Coral Sea in 1989. (PH2 (AW) Wayne Edwards, USN)

THE F/A-18A/B

2

INITIAL HORNETS

Following the selection of the YF-16, McDonnell Douglas and Northrop worked to produce the Model 267, which eventually became the F-18. Despite its physical resemblance to the YF-17, the F-18 was truly a new aircraft. Indeed, it did not share a single dimension with the original YF-17. Nevertheless, it did retain many of the core YF-17 features, such as the dual engines, the LERX, and the twin canted stabilizers.

One of the major engineering concerns was the YF-17's ability to withstand a 24 feet per second descent rate typical of carrier landings. To increase stability during carrier landings and on a pitching deck, the main landing gear were moved further aft to provide a track of 10 feet 2.5 inches (from the 6 feet 10.75 inches of the YF-17), and given a distinctive "L" shape versus their original straight design. The airframe and undercarriage were strengthened considerably

to accommodate the rigors of carrier operations. The nose landing gear was modified to a twin-wheel design with a forward launch bar, and configured to retract forward into the nose section. The main landing gear retracted aft, then rotated through 90 degrees to rest flat underneath the air intake ducts. One complicating factor throughout this redesign was the need for the fuselage stations to facilitate the Sparrow missile and/or sensor (FLIR/NAV) pods.

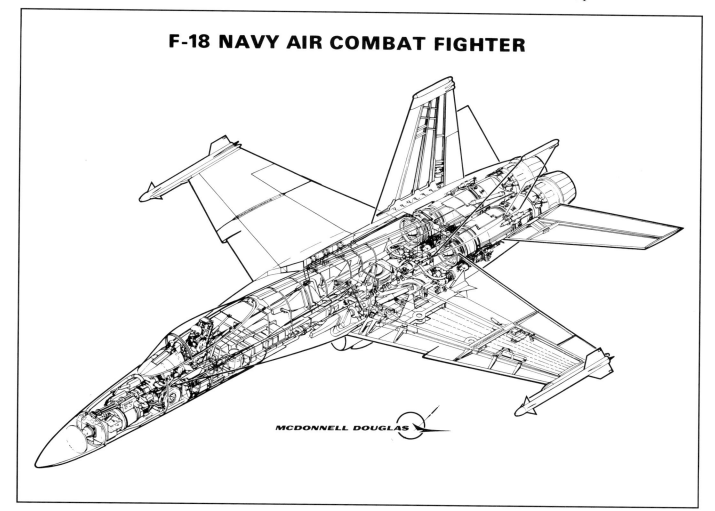

F-18 NAVY AIR COMBAT FIGHTER

This illustration shows the interior of the F-18 Navy Air Combat Fighter. (Boeing)

Here is an artist's rendition of the F-18 and A-18 in their respective roles. The Navy had planned to equip attack (VA) squadrons with the A-18 and fighter squadrons (VF) with the F-18. (Boeing via National Naval Aviation Museum)

Modifications were also made to the fuselage, adding four inches in width to the aft area, enlarging the fuselage spine, and toeing the engines slightly outward. A retractable hose and drogue-capable refueling probe was also added just ahead of the cockpit and on the right. Fuel was carried in four self-sealing fuselage tanks (426, 249, 200, and 530 gallons), and two 96-gallon wing tanks, the latter of which are packed with explosion suppression foam. Overall, the internal fuel capacity was increased from 5,500 lbs. to 10,800 lbs.

The Hornet received the new 16,000-lb. thrust F404-GE-400 turbofan engines, which possessed a more respectable bypass ratio of 0.30. The major difference between F404 and the J79 used by the F-4 was in weight and size; the F404 weighed approximately half the weight of the J79 and was approximately 25 percent smaller. It also contained some 7,700 fewer parts. The F404 proved remarkably responsive and resistant to stall, even during high angles-of-attack. Interestingly, the F404 engines are "neutral" powerplants, meaning that the same engine fits in either engine bay. This is made possible by separating the airframe accessories package from the powerplants, mounting them instead on the airframe. The airframe accessories are mounted on the AMAD. The engine accessories are bottom-mounted on the engine for maintenance and interchangeability.

The F-18's wing area grew from 350 square feet in the YF-17 to 400 square feet, and the wings were two feet longer in span. Chord was also increased to 20 degrees to improve handling characteristics at low speed. To prevent a slight flutter problem discovered during the F-15 flight tests, a small wing "snag" or "dogtooth" discontinuity was added on the leading edge of both the wing flaps and the stabilators. The F-18's stabilators were also enlarged and given a lower aspect ratio. Similar to the YF-17, the fins are canted outward, but at 20 rather than 18 degrees.

All control surfaces were computerized to provide the optimal performance during all flight regimes.

Unlike the YF-17, which relied on three control surfaces (rudders, stabilators, ailerons), the F-18 utilizes five control surfaces: ailerons, leading- and trailing-edge flaps, stabilators, and rudders. Directional control is provided by the rudders, with roll control provided by differential movements of the stabilators, ailerons, and leading- and trailing-edge flaps. Pitch control is obtained by moving the stabilators together.

From a weapons standpoint, the F-18 utilizes nine external stores stations. The two wingtip stations are for the AIM-9 Sidewinder missile or instrument pods. Two stations, rated at 2,500 lbs. and 2,350 lbs. (from inboard to outboard), are also locat-ed under each wing, and can carry additional air-to-air or a variety of air-to-ground munitions. The inboard stations can also carry 300-gallon elliptical fuel tanks. A centerline station, rated at 2,600 lbs., can carry air-to-ground weapons or a fuel tank. One of the innovations of the F-18 program was the conversion of the two fuselage stations into dual weapons and sensor stations. When the aircraft was originally conceived in two variants, the fighter version (F-18) was to carry the AIM-7 Sparrow on the fuselage stations, while the attack variant (A-18) was to carry the Ford Aerospace AAS-38 NITE Hawk FLIR on the right station and the Martin Marietta ASQ-173 LDT/SCAM pod on the left station.

RADAR COMBINES THE F-18/A-18

Because the YF-17 was designed as a pure air-to-air fighter, its Westinghouse radar offered limited range and could not provide illumination for radar-guided weapons such as the Sparrow. With the Navy insisting on a Sparrow missile and 30-nm plus radar range capability, McDonnell Douglas turned to the Hughes (now Raytheon) APG-65 digital multi-mode pulse-Doppler "lookdown, shoot-down" radar. Use of the Hughes radar resulted in an enlargement to the nose radome diameter of approximately four inches to accommodate the larger (28-inch) antenna. The cockpit was also moved back four inches.

The first F-18 took to the skies on 18 November 1975 with Paul Kriggs at the controls. This Hornet was the only preproduction aircraft to sport this colorful paint scheme of white with blue and gold trim. (Boeing)

Indeed, designing a radar compact enough for the limited space allotted in the Hornet (only 4.45 cubic feet) was one of the most challenging aspects of the aircraft's early life. Unlike the large and powerful AWG-9 radar, around which the F-14 was designed, the Hornet's radar had to be designed to fit in the airframe. Overcoming significant technological hurdles, Hughes succeeded not only in producing a compact design (weighing less than 40 percent of the F-15's APG-63), but also by producing a radar that could operate well in both the air-to-air and air-to-ground mode. This proved to be a key point in the F/A-18's evolution, as it allowed one aircraft to perform both the fighter and attack mission without the need to change any systems. All a pilot need do was to flip a switch.

The radar has proven to be reliable and easy to maintain. Rack mounted on rails to accommodate easy access, most of the modules are removable without disturbing the others and the entire radar can be removed and replaced within 12 minutes. The requirements for the APG-65's reliability can no doubt be traced to the poor radar reliability rates experienced by F-4s during Vietnam.

Of the events during this phase of the Hornet program, the ability to merge the two missions into one plane was significant. The F-18 and A-18 had been sold on the idea that two similar airframes would reduce costs by leading to an economy of scale for parts and maintainers; moreover, with the change of a few black boxes, an F-18 could become an A-18 and vice versa. Now, these economies were even more significant because no switch was needed; now the two missions could be flown by the same plane, even on the same flight. This signaled the birth of the true modern-day strike-fighter.

GLASS COCKPIT DESIGN

The compact design of the Hornet's cockpit sprang from several factors, most significant of which were the limited space available in the F-18 but also the need to combine necessary instrumentation for two distinct missions into one usable format. The F-18s cockpit, created by a team of McDonnell Douglas engineers led by Gene Adam, was also revolutionary in that it ushered in the so-called "glass cockpit" design now the standard on military and most commercial aircraft.

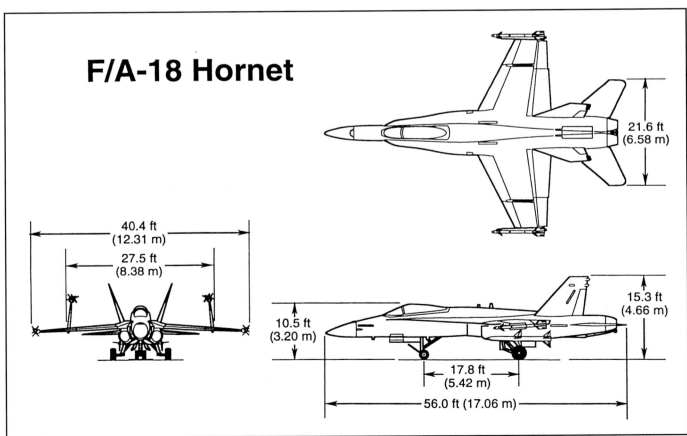

The general arrangement of the F-18 is shown in this diagram. (Boeing)

This interesting formation of VFA-15 Valions *depicts the Hornet's shapes well. Notice how the Sidewinder missiles angle down on their launchers (lower Hornet) and the contoured shape of the LEX (upper Hornet). Both aircraft are carrying a single 330-gallon external tank and no wing pylons are affixed.* (Boeing)

Moving past the old-style gauges and dials of the YF-17 (and even the state-of-the-art F-15A), the Hornet's cockpit features three Digital Display Indicators (DDIs). The DDIs present pilots with a computerized menu allowing them access to literally dozens of pages of information (ranging from threat data to systems checks to radar information) by simply pressing a button and moving deeper into the "book". In the event of a failure, either DDI can display any information selected. The center display offers a color moving map. Directly in front of the pilot is the "up front control" (UFC) console containing the navigation and communications gear. A limited number of back-up gauges and instruments are at the lower right in the event of a computer failure.

Another significant part of the cockpit is the hands-on-throttle-and-stick system, called HOTAS. Using HOTAS, a pilot can control all instruments needed for air combat, thereby dispensing with the need to look inside the cockpit during critical moments. The F/A-18 stick features seven selectors, most dealing with weapons stores controls, weapons firing, and one controlling the radar acquisition modes. The throttles feature ten switches and controls, including as the more significant the chaff/flare dispenser, communications, speed brake, and radar controls. The throttles are dual and have finger lifts enabling the controller to slide into afterburner.

THE F-18 COMES TO LIFE

On 22 January 1976, a $1.43 billion seven-year Full-Scale Development (FSD) contract was signed calling for 11 research & development aircraft, designated as the F-18, and specifying for the first flight by

THE HORNET'S RADAR

The Hughes (now Raytheon) APG-65 was the primary Hornet radar until the mid-1990s when replaced by the much more capable APG-73. The APG-65 is a liquid-cooled, multi-mode pulse-Doppler unit, providing both air-to-air and air-to-ground modes. Operating in the J-band wavelength, the APG-65 uses an interleaved high- and medium-pulse repetition frequency (PRF) to provide all-aspect acquisition. Small and compact, it takes up a mere 4.4 cubic feet of space and weighs just 350 lbs.

For the air-to-air mission, the APG-65 uses four search/track modes for longer range intercepts (out to 100 nm) and four auto acquisition modes for maneuvering in the short-range environment (500 feet to 5 nm). The search/track modes include:

Velocity Search (VS): Utilizing high PRF, this mode can find targets at maximum ranges (up to 100 nm by some reports), but at the expense of details. Speed and bearing information is provided, but not range, and priority is given to contacts with a positive closure rate.

Range-While-Search (RWS): This mode combines high and medium PRF to detect contacts at ranges between 40 and 80 nm regardless of their closure rate or aspect and provide range information while continuing to search for additional contacts. Single-target-track (STT) mode is automatically cued once a contact comes into firing range. STT is the mode for firing the AIM-7 Sparrow, and it relies on two-channel monopulse angle-tracking. Target aspect angles, altitude, and speed are displayed on the radar screen while steering commands and targeting data are displayed on the HUD. A "SHOOT" cue is flashed on the HUD once a firing solution is achieved. The primary drawback of STT is the need to keep the target within the radar's gimbals in order to maintain tracking.

Track-While-Scan (TWS): Using medium PRF, this mode searches out to approximately 40 nm and allows pilots to track targets, while continuing a search scan. Up to ten targets can be tracked with information (aspect angle, speed, altitude) on eight contacts displayed on the radar screen. The "fire-and-forget" AIM-120 AMRAAM is launched from this mode.

The Hughes (later Raytheon) APG-65 radar. (U.S. Navy)

Raid Assessment (RAID): One tactic employed by aircraft is that of flying in close formation to fool enemy radars into believing there is only one contact. This mode, operable to distances of approximately 35 nm, uses Doppler-beam sharpening to scrutinize a specific contact and sort out individual aircraft flying in close formation that might, on other modes, appear as a single contact.

Auto acquisition modes are essentially air combat maneuvering modes that are intended to make targeting easier during the heat of a dogfight. All are to be used where bandits are within 5 miles and these can be accessed from the control stick. In these modes, acquisition is automatic, but pilots have the option to "step through" to the next target, or the one after. These modes include:

Boresight: This projects a narrow scan directly ahead of the Hornet and provides highly accurate range and speed information. Essentially, this is a point-the-plane-and-shoot mode.

Vertical Acquisition (VACQ): To be used in a turning fight, this mode scans through a narrow beam arc from 60 degrees above to 14 degrees below the Hornet's centerline. The Hornet can turn in the target's plane of motion and achieve lock.

HUD mode: This scans through a box projected out from the HUD and measuring 10 degrees left and right of boresight and 14 degrees up, 6 degrees down below foresight. This mode is also called Wide Acquisition or WACQ.

Gun Director: Also a short-range mode, this provides range, aspect, position, and speed information for the gunsight aiming point, or "pipper". Appropriate allowances are made for angle-off and lead.

For air-to-surface missions, a number of highly flexible modes are offered. The Real Beam Ground Mapping (RBGM) mode creates a small map of the terrain ahead and is useful for identifying geographical features, and, hence, navigation. This mode has three sub-modes: Doppler Beam Sharpening (DBS) Sector mode magnifies a selected portion of the map to a ratio of 19:1 and is useful for area identification; DBS Patch mode focuses on an even smaller area with a magnification ratio of 69:1, and helps find small targets; a Synthetic Aperture Radar (SAR) mode provides 30 feet by 60 feet resolution out to approximately 30 nautical miles.

Three air-to-ground modes serve primarily as attack modes. Fixed Target Track (FTT) is used for attacking a fixed target with a significant radar return and uses two-channel monopulse angle-tracking, similar to the STT air-to-air mode. It can be used for direct attack or to establish a navigational waypoint. Ground Moving Target Track (GMTT) mode is similar to FTT, but for use against moving targets on the ground. The Air-to-Surface Ranging (ASR) mode is used to deliver ordnance for dive attacks. It uses either monopulse angle tracking for shallow dive angles, or split-gate range tracking for steep angles. This mode is also used to provide ranging information while using the FLIR or laser designator. Targets at sea are prosecuted using the Sea Surface Search (SSS) mode, which has filters for background clutter. Other air-to-ground modes include Terrain Avoidance, Precision Velocity Update (for precision navigation and weapons aiming).

The Phase I Radar Upgrade (RUG) APG-73 was introduced in May 1994 and brought with it significantly faster processing capabilities. Relying on the latest advances in technologies, the unit weighs the same as the APG-65, but offers a ten-fold increase in processor speed and has greater memory. It is also easier to maintain and more reliable. The APG-73 program began in 1989 under a joint development program with Canada and aimed to improve the APG-65's electronic counter-countermeasures (ECCM) system. While it uses the same antenna and transmitter as the APG-65, the APG-73 incorporates all new electronics. Following its first flight on 15 April 1992, the APG-73 became standard on all production models (beginning with Lot XVI) and the radars were retrofitted into older models. VFA-146 and -147 were the first Hornet squadrons to receive the upgraded units. As they were removed from the Hornets, the APG-65 radars have been installed in the AV-8B+ Harrier.

The APG-73 is also used by the F/A-18E/F, discussed later. It has the same modes as the APG-65. The RUG Phase II incorporates a high-resolution SAR for mapping during reconnaissance missions and autonomous targeting for the JSOW and JDAM weapons. It also allows tracking of up to 24 targets. RUG Phase II units are used only by Marine Corps F/A-18Ds and several participated in Operation Allied Force.

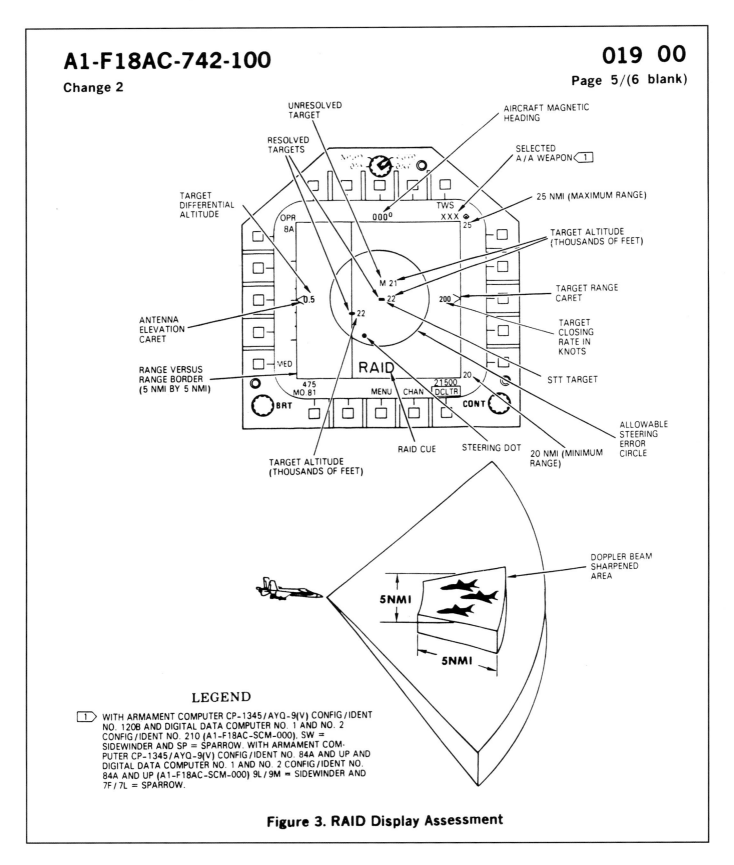

Figure 3. RAID Display Assessment

LEGEND

1 ▷ WITH ARMAMENT COMPUTER CP-1345/AYQ-9(V) CONFIG/IDENT
NO. 120B AND DIGITAL DATA COMPUTER NO. 1 AND NO. 2
CONFIG/IDENT NO. 210 (A1-F18AC-SCM-000), SW =
SIDEWINDER AND SP = SPARROW. WITH ARMAMENT COM-
PUTER CP-1345/AYQ-9(V) CONFIG/IDENT NO. 84A AND UP AND
DIGITAL DATA COMPUTER NO. 1 AND NO. 2 CONFIG/IDENT NO.
84A AND UP (A1-F18AC-SCM-000) 9L/9M = SIDEWINDER AND
7F/7L = SPARROW.

The raid assessment mode was introduced by the APG-65 allowing pilots to isolate contacts and decipher whether there are multiple, but hidden aircraft within a single blip. (F-18 NATOPS via Dennis R. Jenkins)

July 1978. Just months earlier, General Electric had been awarded a contract to develop the F404 turbofan engine, a subtle predictor of the F-18 contract to come. There were eventually to be three versions: the F-18 fighter for the Navy and Marine Corps; the A-18 attack variant, for the Navy; and the TF-18, a dual-seat trainer for the Navy. The TF-18 would also retain a basic armament capability.

Despite the fact that the YF-17 was entirely a Northrop design, it was agreed that the F-18 would be produced through a partnership between McDonnell Douglas and Northrop using a 60/40 split. McDonnell Douglas manufactured the wings, stabilators, and forward fuselage area, while Northrop produced the center and aft fuselage sections, and the vertical stabilizers. Northrop's rear fuselage assemblies were then shipped to St. Louis where they were mated with the wings and forward fuselage, and final test flights were conducted. McDonnell Douglas' extra 20 percent essentially represented the final assembly production aspects, and the fact that it was the team leader. Tolerances between the two plants were fixed at 0.002 inches in order to insure compatibility.

On 1 March 1977, the F-18 was named the "Hornet." The initial contract called for the production of 780 F-18s for Navy fighter and attack as well as Marine Corps squadrons.

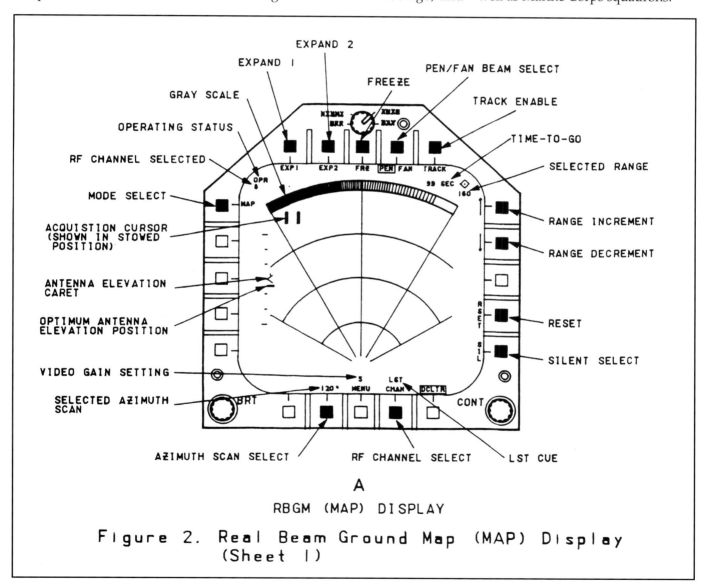

A
RBGM (MAP) DISPLAY

Figure 2. Real Beam Ground Map (MAP) Display (Sheet 1)

Ground mapping is another important radar display and is used during ground attack missions and for navigation. (F-18 NATOPS via Dennis R. Jenkins)

ROLL OUT AND FIRST FLIGHT

The first F/A-18 (BuNo. 160775) was rolled out of McDonnell Douglas' St. Louis facility on 13 September 1978 and took to the skies on its maiden flight on 18 November. McDonnell Douglas test pilot John E. "Jack" Krings was at the controls. The flight, which lasted approximately 50 minutes, saw the aircraft fly from St. Louis, Missouri, northeast to Springfield, Illinois, and back, reaching a top speed of 300 knots and an altitude of 24,000 feet. Krings described the aircraft as remarkably stable and a pleasure to fly.

Following additional tests in St. Louis, the F/A-18 underwent a regime of flight tests at the Naval Air Test Center (NATC) Patuxent River beginning in January 1979, which lasted through October 1982. YF/A-18 No. 2 first flew on 12 March 1979, and the last prototype, No. 11, made its initial flight in March 1980. Unlike the flight test and development programs of other aircraft of the day, almost all of the Hornet's testing was conducted at Patuxent River. This system, known as the Principal Site Concept, incorporated substantial input from the Navy and also allotted more time for McDonnell Douglas to incorporate modifications and to fix deficiencies. Moreover, it kept virtually all of the Hornets together at one test location, reducing logistics problems.

TEST FLIGHTS REVEAL PROBLEMS

Given its similar configuration to the YF-17, which had undergone extensive testing, including as much as 5,000 wind tunnel hours and the LWF competition, many expected the F-18s flight test phase to proceed without a hitch. Yet, as is often the case in flight test programs, the F-18 had glitches that had to be solved. In fact, some of the problems were of such degree that the wing and the tail section had to be partially redesigned. As a testament to the prowess of their engineering departments, McDonnell Douglas and Northrop resolved virtually all of these "deficiencies" during the flight test program and rapidly incorporated these modifications into the production aircraft.

Of these deficiencies, the most significant were those associated with the Hornet's range and roll-rate.

HORNET FULL-SCALE DEVELOPMENT AIRCRAFT

All 11 of the FSD aircraft were assigned to the flight test program, with the individual aircraft assuming the following program duties:

BuNo.	Aircraft	Test Function
160775	YF/A-18A No. 1	basic flight and flutter exploration
160776	YF/A-18A No. 2	propulsion and performance
160777	YF/A-18A No. 3	carrier suitability and ECS (environmental control system)
160778	YF/A-18A No. 4	structural flight test; back-up non-flying static and fatigue articles
160779	YF/A-18A No. 5	full avionics and weapons systems
160780	YF/A-18A No. 6	high AOA and spin recovery testing
160781	YF/A-18B No. T1	clearing configuration; air-to-air armament systems
160782	YF/A-18A No. 7	armament systems
160783	YF/A-18A No. 8	performance and systems; first gun test
160784	YF/A-18B No. T2	F404 accelerated engine service life
160785	YF/A-18A No. 9	maintenance engineering and electromagnetic compatibility

The testing was structured such that each prototype introduced at least one new modification or system/structural change resulting from prior flight-testing or ground research. During the test flight program, the 11 Hornets accumulated 3,583 flight hours in 2,756 flights.

This underside photo depicts a rather large weapons load of four Mk 83 1,000-lb. bombs, three 315-gallon elliptical tanks, an ASQ-173 Laser Spot Tracker (LST) on the right fuselage station, a AAS-38 FLIR on the left fuselage station, and two wingtip-mounted Sidewinders. Demonstrating that the range criticisms were not as bad as critics claimed, this aircraft flew 1,240 miles from NAS Patuxent River, Maryland, to strike targets in Florida, then returned to base for refueling, and still had enough gas for two passes at the field. (via Robert F. Dorr)

Elliptical fuel tanks capable of holding 315-gallons were initially used on the F-18, but were prone to fatigue cracks and provided too much drag. An AIM-7 is also visible on the fuselage station. This photo further shows a good view of the modified main landing gear.
(Robert Lawson via
National Naval Aviation Museum)

These deficiencies came as a serious blow to the Navy/McDonnell Douglas/Northrop/Raytheon/GE team, and provided cannon fodder for the political pundits and the aviation media community. During flight tests at 10,000 feet, roll rates were experienced of 185 degrees per second at Mach 0.7, 160 degrees per second at Mach 0.8, and 100 degrees per second at Mach 0.9. These rates further diminished at higher altitudes, especially near the speed of sound.

Analysis proved that these rates were caused by the outer wings being flexed in high load situations and the Sidewinders, when attached on their wingtip stations, imparting too much roll dampening. The first cause was addressed by strengthening the wing spar and eliminating the dogtooth on the leading-edge wing flap. The ailerons were also extended out to the wingtip to provide more deflection, and the leading-edge flaps were split so they could operate independently. Composite skins were also thickened, thereby improving wing rigidity and reducing twist. The angle of the Sidewinder rail was altered of the aircraft during subsonic flight. To resolve this, the wingtip launchers were moved forward by five inches and angled to an even sharper nose-down incidence.

All in all, these modifications brought the roll rate up to an acceptable 220 degrees per second, although still short of the initial 280 degrees per second established earlier by the Navy. Moreover, the changes necessary to correct the problems consumed some five months of the program. F/A-18 No. 8 was the first to receive the wing modifications and all Hornets manufactured after No. 17 were built with the strengthened wing, adding a mere 142 lbs. to the aircraft's overall weight.

Related to the roll rate problem was the considerable time required for the aircraft to accelerate from Mach 0.8 through Mach 1.6. At altitudes of 35,000 feet, the Hornet took a full 180 seconds to accomplish this feat, a far cry from the 110 seconds guaranteed by McDonnell Douglas and even the 120 seconds of the F-4 that the F/A-18 was intended to replace. Changes to the flight control system resulted in acceleration times of less than 120 seconds, although not as low as the 80-second requirement desired by the Navy.

The original nose gear of the YF-17 were beefed up and a second wheel added to withstand the abuse of carrier landings. Here a Hornet from VFA-113 readies for launch from USS Constellation. *A single Mk 83 bomb is visible on the centerline station.* (U.S. Navy)

The range problem was equally perplexing, but more difficult to solve, and, indeed, is not fully resolved to this day. The Hornet suffered a 12 percent deficiency in range during flight tests. Navy requirements had called for a range of 444 nms when configured as a fighter and 635 nms when configured as an attack aircraft. Initial tests placed these figures, though, at 400 and 580 nms. In 1982, the range limitations were highlighted by VX-5's test report which cited shortcomings in the F/A-18 as a replacement for the A-7, citing range and endurance deficiencies. Some Navy officials responded sharply to the report, noting that the tests were based on faulty profiles. "The aircraft are different," one official noted. "If you force the F/A-18 to fly the same profiles that are optimum for the A-7 it will perform poorly. However, the F/A-18 does as well or better when flown properly." These comments were backed up by numbers accumulated by VFA-125 as it worked with the Hornet. Indeed, some people familiar with the Hornet's early years contend that the test pilots, many of whom were former A-4, A-6, and A-7 pilots, simply flew the Hornet out of profile.

Several other electronic and flight control causes for the range deficiency were also discovered. The leading-edge flaps, for example, were found to be 2 to 3 degrees down and the LEX slots increased drag. Changes in the flight control system moved the flaps to 0 position in regular flight. The LEX slots were partially filled, leaving only a small slot aft of the cockpit to funnel fuselage bleed air away from the intakes. In fleet use, the range "problem" has been minimized, as the fleet has discovered many ways

An AIM-9 on station 9 is shown here. The drooped partial aileron indicates that this photo was taken in the early 1980s, before the changes were incorporated to increase roll-rate. The ailerons were extended out to the wingtips and programmed to extend to 45 degrees during certain flight regimes. (Boeing)

to reduce or eliminate fuel concerns, including fuel consumption measures, use of organic tanking, and proper mission planning.

Other problems developed which, although serious, posed less concerns. For example, F/A-18s experienced a high nose wheel lift-off speed of around 140 knots. Optimally, the nose should have lifted at about 100 knots. However, this deficiency was resolved by eliminating the dogtooth snag located on the stabilator and by programming the flight control computers to toe-in the rudders at 25 degrees during take-off. The toe-in provided an extra push down on the aft fuselage, resulting in a new lift-off speed of 115 knots.

Carrier qualifications were another area where deficiencies initially appeared. Following a stint over several weeks at Patuxent River, where F/A-18 No. 3 completed 70

land catapult launches and 120 arrested landings, the aircraft departed for USS *America* in the Atlantic for initial sea trials. The trials lasted from 30 October through 3 November and tallied 32 launches and traps, 17 touch-and-go landings, and approximately 14 hours of flight time. Of the 32 arrested recoveries, the pilots caught the targeted third wire 24 times.

Although the aircraft performed well, a deficiency was discovered in the aircraft's approach speed that caused alarm. The requirements had called for a 115 to 125 knot approach speed with no wind over deck (WOD). The Hornet had posted approach speeds of approximately 140 knots. The solution was found by configuring the leading-edge flaps to 30 degrees and the trailing-edge flaps to 45 degrees of depression. This change, coupled with a software modification, reduced the approach

Production Hornets feature full span flaps. This Canadian CF-188 is shown at rest, with flaps and ailerons drooped to de-stress the hydraulic system. (Brad Elward)

(imbedded with aluminum) composition, and presented more drag than anticipated. These were replaced with conventional all-aluminum 330-gallon circular tanks. A host of smaller problems were also revealed, all of which were resolved before the Hornet entered production. In the end, the Hornet met 17 of the 20 design goals. More importantly, of the three that missed mark – range, approach speed, and maximum gross weight – the discrepancies were minor and have all been accommodated by fleet experience with the aircraft.

THE TWO-PLACE F/A-18B

speed to approximately 134 knots where it remains today. In fact, top hook honors given following carrier deployments are generally awarded to Hornet pilots, which suggests that this faster than desired approach speed is not really a problem.

A minor flutter with the underwing pylons developed during weapons

trials, which was eliminated by moving the stores rack forward five inches and by changing the flight control software to make the landing flaps "beat" against the lateral oscillation caused by heavy stores weights on the pylons. The elliptical 300-gallon (and later 315-gallon) fuel tanks also suffered fatigue problems, due in part to their spun fiber

As the dual-role redesignation occurred, the TF-18 became the F/A-18B. The primary differences between the A and B model were the two cockpits and the associated larger canopy. To accommodate the second person, the forward-most fuel bladder was removed, reducing the overall fuel capacity by just six percent less than the single-seat model.

VMFA-314's **Black Knights** *were the first operational Hornet squadron in January 1983.* (Don Linn)

The aft cockpit featured a separate stick and throttle, but lacked an HUD and a hook control. F/A-18Bs have been used almost exclusively by the various FRS squadrons to train new Hornet pilots and by VAQ-34, the Navy's now disestablished electronic aggressor squadron.

Interestingly, it was the Marines, and not the Navy that recognized the two-place Hornet's potential as a tactical aircraft, and later adopted the F/A-18D in that role, replacing the retired A-6Es. The Navy was unable to follow suit, because no tests had ever been conducted as to the F/A-18B's carrier suitability. Some have commented that this was intentional, as the Navy did not want to be perceived as challenging the F-14's territory. Moreover, to qualify the B for carrier operations was inconsistent with the sales pitch that the LWF was a complement to, and not a replacement for, the F-14. Later, the potential of the two-seat Super Hornet for carrier operations was foreshadowed by using the F/A-18F for the carrier suitability portion of the EMD.

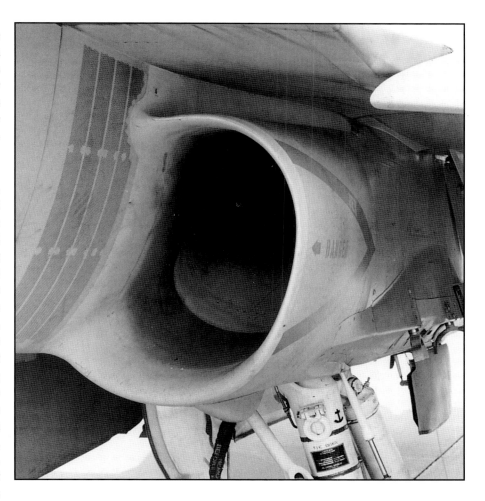

The Hornet's engine intakes are D-shaped. The small fairing underneath the intake houses an ALR-67 antenna. Not visible, but just aft of the fairing is an ALE-39 countermeasures dispenser. (Brad Elward)

F/A-18A/B OPERATIONAL HISTORY

VFA-125, the first F/A-18 Fleet Readiness Squadron (FRS), was commissioned at NAS Lemoore, California, on 13 November 1980, and received its first Hornets three months later, and then began training the new instructors who would, in turn, train F/A-18 fleet units. The squadron received its first production Hornet in September and spent much of the following year developing and preparing the new training syllabus. Flying two-place F/A-18Bs, VFA-125 crews underwent a short carrier qualification aboard *Constellation* and accumulated 57 day and 24 night traps and 10 bolters. Since

VFA-125 was to serve both the Navy and Marine Corps in training Hornet pilots and maintainers, it was manned from the start as a joint service squadron, with equal numbers of men from each service on the staff.

On 7 January 1983, the first Hornet squadron, VMFA-314 at MCAS El Toro, California, was declared operational; VMFAs-323 and -531 followed shortly thereafter. The first Navy squadrons to receive the F/A-18A were VFA-25 and -113 of Air Wing 14. These two squadrons would later make the Hornets first operational deployment aboard *Constellation* during 1985. A second FRS, VFA-106, stood up at NAS Cecil

Field, the East Coast F/A-18 base, on 27 April 1984.

Interestingly, the first three East Coast F/A-18 squadrons, VFA-131, -132, and -136, were all commissioned at NAS Lemoore, then transferred to Cecil Field. Two of these squadrons, VFA-131, and -132, along with VMFA 314 and -323, were assigned to CVW-13 aboard USS *Coral Sea* (CV 43) and saw the Hornet's first combat in 1986 during the Operation *Prairie Fire* (24 March through 14 April) and *El Dorado Canyon* (15 April) raids against Libya in retaliation for a terrorist attack in Berlin, Germany. HARM-equipped F/A-18s flew Suppression of Enemy

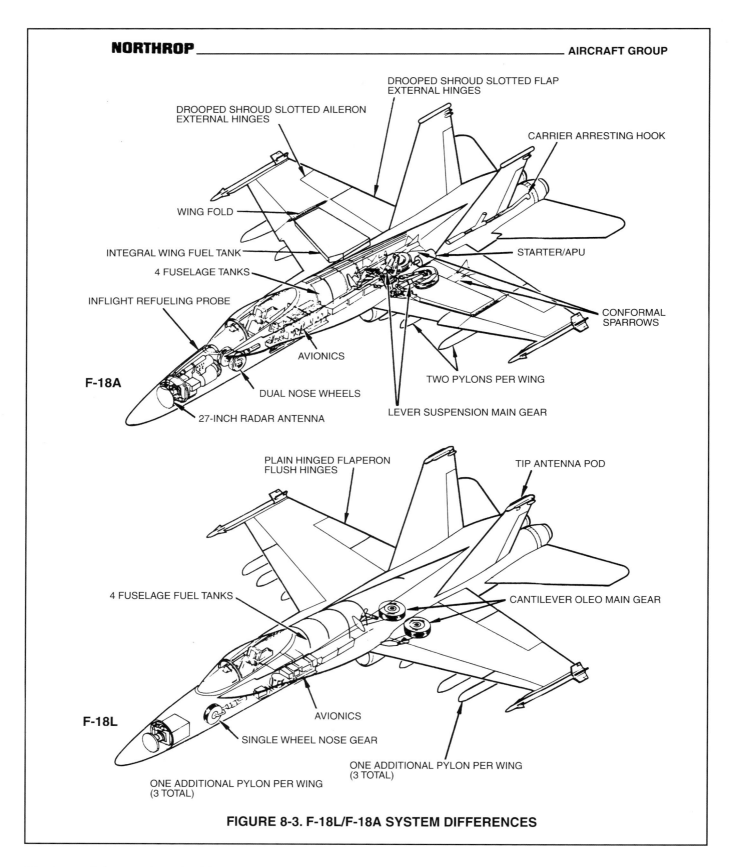

DROOPED SHROUD SLOTTED FLAP
EXTERNAL HINGES

DROOPED SHROUD SLOTTED AILERON
EXTERNAL HINGES

CARRIER ARRESTING HOOK

WING FOLD

INTEGRAL WING FUEL TANK

4 FUSELAGE TANKS

STARTER/APU

INFLIGHT REFUELING PROBE

CONFORMAL
SPARROWS

AVIONICS

F-18A

TWO PYLONS PER WING

DUAL NOSE WHEELS

LEVER SUSPENSION MAIN GEAR

27-INCH RADAR ANTENNA

PLAIN HINGED FLAPERON
FLUSH HINGES

TIP ANTENNA POD

4 FUSELAGE FUEL TANKS

CANTILEVER OLEO MAIN GEAR

F-18L

AVIONICS

SINGLE WHEEL NOSE GEAR

ONE ADDITIONAL PYLON PER WING
(3 TOTAL)

ONE ADDITIONAL PYLON PER WING
(3 TOTAL)

FIGURE 8-3. F-18L/F-18A SYSTEM DIFFERENCES

Northrop tried to market a land-based variant of the F-18 dubbed the F-18L. This diagram depicts the physical differences between the two. No interest was shown in Northrop's product. (Northrop via Dennis R. Jenkins)

Air Defenses (SEAD) missions, while other air wing Hornets flew Surface Combat Air Patrol (Sur-CAP) and fleet defense, the latter protecting the U.S. battlegroup against Libyan MiG-23 and Su-22 attack planes that were sortieing to monitor U.S. actions. A third Hornet FRS, VMFAT-101, was established at MCAS El Toro in 1987 with the task of training new Marine pilots, Weapons Systems Operators (WSOs), and maintainers.

A total of 371 F/A-18As and 39 F/A-18Bs were built through mid-1987. The F/A-18A still serves in one active-duty Navy (VFA-97) and two Marine Corps (VMFA-115, -122) squadrons, although by 2003 these should be withdrawn from service. The F/A-18A has also been flown by reserve squadrons, various test facilities, and also by NASA, whose work has concentrated on testing high angles-of-attack vehicles (HARV) and thrust-vectored engines. The *Blue Angels*, the Navy's Flight Demonstration Team, adopted the F/A-18A in November 1986, replacing the A-4F Skyhawk which had served the *Blue Angels* well since 1974. The team operates nine F/A-18As and two F/A-18B, all of which were non-deployable Lot IVs at first, but have since been changed to Lot VIs. F/A-18A/Bs are being upgraded through Engineering Change Proposal (ECP) 560/583 to keep the aircraft capable until 2010+ and add AIM-120 and FLIR capability, new computers, and the APG-73 radar.

The Gulf of Sidra provided the Hornet with its first taste of combat during early 1986 when U.S. forces struck terrorist facilities in Libya. This VFA-131 Wildcat CAG-bird is shown escorting a Libyan MiG-23 Flogger in February 1986. (U.S. Navy via National Naval Aviation Museum)

This VMFA-134 vertical tailfin shows an electronic countermeasures antenna (top), a radar warning antenna (lower), and a three-segment formation light. The top fairing on the starboard fin was a position light. These fairings were larger than those of early model F/A-18A/Bs. The bottom, flattish fairing is a fuel vent dump. Also, the three small rectangles just aft and below of the squadron emblem are stiffeners (called doublers) added to hold fatigue cracks that developed. (Ted Carlson)

OPERATION DESERT STORM

Although Operation El Dorado Canyon in 1986 provided the Hornet with its first taste of combat, the true test came in the prolonged air campaign of 1991 that sought to expel Saddam Hussein's Iraqi forces from neighboring Kuwait. Immediately following Iraq's 2 August 1990 invasion of Kuwait, four Navy F/A-18 squadrons and their accompanying air wings were tasked with protecting Saudi installations from an anticipated Iraqi drive to the south. VFA-25 and -113 flew with CVW-15 aboard USS *Independence* in the Persian Gulf and VFA-131 and -136 were with CVW-7 aboard USS *Eisenhower* in the Red Sea. Both carriers departed from the future war zone by September, and were replaced by a total of nine U.S. Navy and seven U.S. Marine Corps F/A-18 squadrons.

Participating U.S. Navy squadrons included: VFA-82 and VFA-86 (both F/A-18C) aboard USS *America* (CV 66); VFA-151, VFA-192, and VFA-195 (all F/A-18A) aboard USS *Midway* (CV 41); VFA-15 and VFA-87 (both F/A-18A) aboard USS *Roosevelt* (CVN-71); VFA-81 and VFA-83 (both F/A-18A) aboard USS *Saratoga* (CV 62). Marine Corps Hornets included: VMFA-314, VMFA-333, and VMFA-451, all flying F/A-18As; VMFA-212, VFMA-232, and VMFA-235 all flew F/A-18Cs; and VFMA(AW)-121 operated the F/A-18D.

Perhaps the Hornet's greatest moment occurred on 17 January 1991, when two F/A-18s from USS *Saratoga* shot down two Iraqi MiG-21 fighters while the Hornets were en route to attack airfield H3 in western Iraq. LCDR Mark Fox (in F/A-18C BuNo. 163508/AA-401) downed one MiG with an

LCDR Mark Fox of VFA-81 poses with the aircraft he flew when he downed an Iraqi MiG-21 during Operation Desert Storm. LCDR Fox is now a Captain and has served as the Commanding Officer. (DoD)

AIM-9, while LT Nick Mongillo (in F/A-18C BuNo. 163502/AA-410) got his kill with an AIM-9, although he fired one Sparrow that failed to track. Both men then went on to complete their mission and bombed their respective targets. This incident indeed demonstrated the true strike-fighter concept at work and validated what Hornet proponents had been preaching for years.

Hornets flew a wide variety of missions, with most Navy missions divided equally between strike (36 percent), general support (34 percent), and fleet defense (30 percent). Early missions saw Hornets flying strike escort and fleet defense, but these soon moved to strike missions as air superiority was obtained. Marine Corps missions focused almost exclusively on close air support (84 percent), followed by general support (16 percent). VMFA(AW)-121's F/A-18Ds were heavily tasked in the FAC role. During the war, Hornets used a variety of ordnance, including Mk 80-series iron bombs, AGM-62 Walleye, AGM-84E SLAM, AGM-65 Maverick, AGM-88 HARM, and Zuni rockets. Approximately 11,179 of the munitions delivered by Hornets were unguided weapons; only 368 guided munitions were delivered.

By the war's end, Hornets had accumulated 11,000 sorties and more than 30,000 flight hours. Total tonnage delivered amounted to 5,513 tons, although this average only 0.74 tons per day per plane. One of the biggest drawbacks was the Hornet airframe's lack of an organic laser designator. Only four AAS-38A pods were available during the war and all were committed to VMFA(AW)-121. This deficiency has since been remedied and all F/A-18 squadrons deploy with the latest variant, the AAS-38B. Hornets achieved a full mission capable rate (FMC) of 90.4 percent during the war and a mission capable rate of 91.5 percent. However, no missions were missed due to maintenance problems, which is remarkable considering the high usage rate. In fact, during one month of the war, the *Saratoga's* air wing reported a usage rate of 128.5 hours per aircraft and turn-around times of less than 30 minutes. Despite the high number of missions, only two Hornets were lost and eight damaged. One was so severely damaged that it flew 35 minutes without oil pressure.

Approximately 30 Canadian CF-188 Hornets also flew in support of Operation Desert Storm. Hornets from Nos. 409, 416, and 439 Squadrons deployed to Doha, Qatar, logging a total of 5,730 flight hours with no losses. Canadian Hornets flew a variety of combat air patrols, escort, and strike missions, and even delivered a small number of laser-guided munitions with the help of Navy A-6E Intruders.

F/A-18Bs were used by the training squadrons, but also by VAQ-34, the West Coast electronic aggressor squadron. Charged with simulating the electronic profile of enemy missiles using electronic pods, these Hornets provided a valuable service to Navy ships. VAQ-34 was disestablished in 1993. (PH1 David Uruse, USN via National Naval Aviation Museum)

The Hornet's internal gun, the GE M61A1 20-mm cannon, has a 578-round capacity and can fire at either 4,000 or 6,000 rounds per minute. The cannon is angled up 2 degrees to enhance its effectiveness in the air-to-air arena. (Ted Carlson)

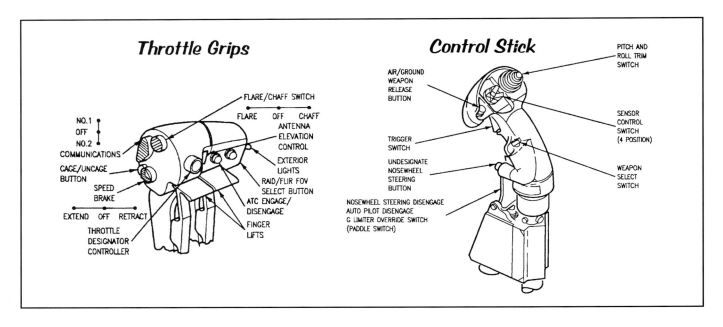

Throttle Grips

- FLARE/CHAFF SWITCH
- FLARE OFF CHAFF
- ANTENNA ELEVATION CONTROL
- NO.1 OFF NO.2 COMMUNICATIONS
- CAGE/UNCAGE BUTTON
- SPEED BRAKE
- EXTEND OFF RETRACT
- THROTTLE DESIGNATOR CONTROLLER
- EXTERIOR LIGHTS
- RAID/FLIR FOV SELECT BUTTON
- ATC ENGAGE/ DISENGAGE
- FINGER LIFTS

Control Stick

- PITCH AND ROLL TRIM SWITCH
- AIR/GROUND WEAPON RELEASE BUTTON
- SENSOR CONTROL SWITCH (4 POSITION)
- TRIGGER SWITCH
- UNDESIGNATE NOSEWHEEL STEERING BUTTON
- WEAPON SELECT SWITCH
- NOSEWHEEL STEERING DISENGAGE AUTO PILOT DISENGAGE G LIMITER OVERRIDE SWITCH (PADDLE SWITCH)

These two drawings show the controls available on the Hornet's HOTAS stick and throttle. (F/A-18C NATOPS)

The Hornet also uses a single-point refueling system, located on the right side of the forward fuselage where it will not interfere with cockpit ingress/egress or access to the radar and gun pallet. (U.S. Navy)

Access to the cockpit is gained via a retractable ladder that folds into the left LEX. A small strut extending up into the well and a "V" brace are provided for additional support. (Brad Elward)

WARBIRD**TECH**
S E R I E S

Due to the Hornet's range limitations, it is almost unheard of that a Hornet will operate without at least one external fuel tank. These tanks can be carried on both inboard stations and the centerline mount using SUU-62 pylon adaptors. The Navy and Marines use the 330-gallon tanks for carrier operations, although both a 480-gallon and 660-gallon tank have been tested for land-based use. At least one photograph has been spotted with a Hornet carrying five tanks; however, the two outboard stations lack plumbing. This Hornet is from VMFA-134. (Ted Carlson)

The fixed ramp intake satisfies all engine airflow needs throughout the flight envelope. The three gray bars on the splitter plate are boundary layer bleed slots. (Ted Carlson)

The Lockheed Martin (Martin Marietta) ASQ-173 laser detector tracker/strike camera (LDT/SCAM) is a derivative of the AAS-35 Pave Penny used by the Air Force's A-10 Thunderbolt II. Carried on the right fuselage station, the ASQ-173 provides accurate bombing information for daytime weapons delivery during poor weather, but affords no night capability. Hornets using the ASQ-173 must rely on "buddy lasing" whereby other laser-designating aircraft, such as the A-6E Intruder, illuminate their targets. The ASQ-173 also features a KB-35A 35-mm strike-recording camera located in the pods aft section, which is used for post-flight bomb damage assessment. The KB-35A has a 35-degree FOV and is panned 180 degrees along the aircraft's track. The pod, however, has largely been replaced by the self-designating AAS-38A/B. (top: Ted Carlson; left: Rick Morgan)

WARBIRDTECH
S E R I E S

The F/A-18C/D

By the mid-1980s it had become clear that the Hornet was a good overall platform and that it was very flexible. The Hornet airframe offered ample room for growth, both in avionics and in systems space, which allowed designers to continually add new and improved avionics systems and weaponry. What followed proved to be the ultimate development in the Hornet line: the F/A-18C/D. Indeed, the C/D is the definite Hornet model through which the aircraft's true capability emerged.

THE FIRST STEP

With the exception of a few new antenna blisters, the F/A-18C looks externally much like the F/A-18A. Internally, however, the aircraft are very different. Moreover, from a mission standpoint, the F/A-18C covers a much broader spectrum, which offers the fleet considerably more flexibility as a weapons platform. Today, F/A-18Cs provide carrier air wings with the full spectrum of air-to-air and air-to-ground missions.

The F/A-18C began as an Engineering Change Proposal (ECP-178) to the F/A-18A to incorporate the newest electronic countermeasures (ALQ-65), a new data link (JTDS), and the laser Maverick weapon. A host of lessor performance-enhancing changes were also packaged into this ECP, which had high Navy priority. The Hornet had been selected as the lead aircraft to employ ALQ-165. A decision was made to redesignate the aircraft to the C model to facilitate logistical support in the fleet.

Ironically, none of the three driving additions ever entered full Navy use, and the ancillary additional changes in the ECP became the essence of the new configuration. Most of the changes ushered in with the C model were software related. A substantially upgraded stores management system and armament system were added and a new flight incident recorder system, and the mission computer was upgraded to the XN-6 (and later the XN-8). This

A VFA-131 Wildcats Hornet from USS George Washington (CVN-73) flies in the "no-fly" zone over southern Iraq during early 1996 with four AMRAAMs and two wingtip-mounted Sidewinders. (LT Tom Haeussler, USN via Rick Burgess)

latter improvement brought with it a three-fold increase in processing speed and twice the memory of the XN-5 used by the F/A-18A. Hardware included a revised Martin-Baker NACES ejection seat.

Externally, a host of new antennas were added, with a Sanders ALQ-126B/165 high-band transmit antenna and an ALQ-165 low-band receiver ECM antenna installed on the trailing-edge of each vertical stabilizer, and an ALQ-165 on the leading-edge of each LEX and above the formation lights. Antennas for the ALR-67 radar warning receiver were also added to the fuselage: a low-band array under the nose, an antenna on either side

of the nose barrel, and on the trailing edge of each vertical stabilizer.

Production began in mid-1987 and the first production F/A-18C (BuNo. 163427) flew on 3 September 1987 piloted by Glen Larson. The OPEVAL that followed was short and turned up no surprises, although fuel deficiencies continued. VFA-25 and -113, the same Navy squadrons that received the first Hornets back in 1983, took deliveries of the first C models in June 1989. A total of 137 F/A-18Cs were built before the line switched to the more capable night attack variant discussed below. The F/A-18D brought to the two-seat version the same modifications and improvements as the C along with a

"decoupled and convertible" aft cockpit to facilitate combat use of the D for either pilot training or for a Naval flight officer in back instead of a pilot. The first 31 of this new model were assigned to the Navy and Marine Corps training squadrons to fill the role of the F/A-18B.

NIGHT ATTACK HORNETS BRING FORTH NEW CAPABILITIES

Beginning with Fiscal Year 1988, all production C/Ds were manufactured as fully night-capable platforms and given the name Night Attack Hornets. Key to this upgrade was the GEC-Marconi AXS-9 (MXV-810) Cat Eyes night vision goggles (NVGs), two new Kaiser 5-inch by

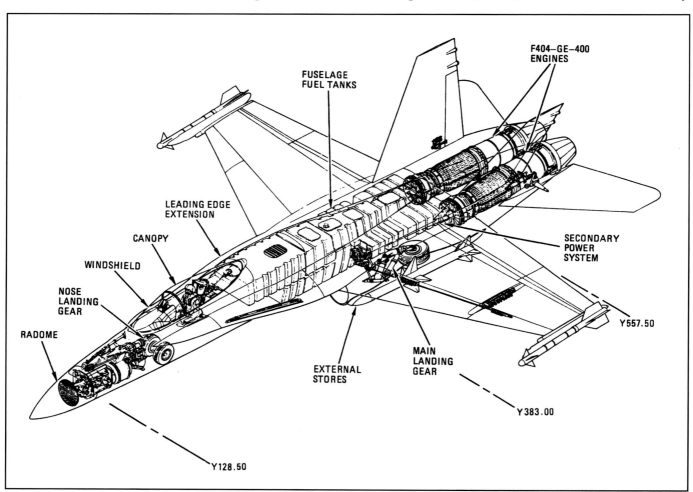

The general arrangement of the F/A-18. (F/A-18C NATOPS via Dennis R. Jenkins)

5-inch color MFDs, and a Smiths Srs 2100 color digital moving map display. Also added was Raytheon's AAR-50 navigation FLIR (NAVFLIR) to be used on all night-attack models to provide night-time navigation imagery overlaid on the HUD. The NAVFLIR pod, also called the Thermal Imaging Navigation Set, or TINS, was mounted on the right fuselage station and provided imagery that could be projected onto the HUD in one-to-one scale as well as on the MFD. The TINS presented a 19-degree field of view, but offered no designation or tracking capability. A gold-tinted canopy was also added to help deflect radar and laser energy away from the cockpit.

The Night Attack F/A-18D models are used by the Marine Corps for all-weather attack aircraft, assuming the mission once flown by the A-6E. Most of the modifications to the two-place D are to the aft cockpit, which formerly housed a second set of flight controls for training. All Ds, including the early ones before Night Attack, were delivered with a conversion kit to permit reconfiguring between stick and throttle (for an instructor) or hand-held controllers (for an NFO).

VMFA(AW)-121 received the first D on 11 May 1990 and flew missions over Iraq during Operation Desert Storm. Marine Corps F/A-18Ds flew both attack and Forward Air Controller-Airborne (FAC-A) missions over geographic grid "kill" boxes. The aircraft have also been active in United Nations operations over Bosnia and Kosovo. During the Spring 1999 *Allied Force* air campaign against Yugoslavia, two Marine F/A-18D(RC)s from VFMA(AW)-332 deployed to Tazar, Hungary, with their new ATARS reconnaissance system and flew

An F/A-18D from VMFA(AW)-223 Vikings *fires a single Zuni during an exercise near NAS Fallon, Nevada in 1991.* (Boeing)

combined reconnaissance/strike missions against Yugoslavian forces. The last F/A-18D was presented to VMFA(AW)-121 on 25 August 2000, marking the end of the Hornet production line.

Applicable to all Night Attack configured Hornets and retrofitted into all C/Ds and some A/Bs is a new sensor fusion software package. This package integrates surveillance, tracking, and identification data gathered from the aircraft's radar, infrared, and ESM sensors to improve situational awareness and reduce pilot workload in the air-to-air arena. Called "Multi-Source Integration", or MSI software, the system coordinates or "fuses" information concerning a target's range, speed, line-of-sight angles, electronic emissions, and other parameters, to ensure better missile delivery accuracy. CDR Jeff Crutchfield, then chief NAWS-China Lake test pilot, explained this fusion in 1992, stating

"We get the best range from the radar, but line-of-sight information is much tighter from a FLIR." This improves standoff target recognition, targeting accuracy, while at the same time reducing the pilot's workload.

Instead of having to look at three or four sensor "inputs", Hornet pilots can now monitor a single display of track files from all sensors, all of which are tracking the same target. The MSI system also improves the Hornet's vulnerability to countermeasures systems and harsh maneuvering. For example, if a targeted aircraft's onboard jammers "break" a radar lock, targeting might then be provided by the FLIR. The Hornet was the first U.S. tactical aircraft to receive this technology.

SUBSEQUENT C/D UPGRADES

Although the Night Attack variant was introduced in 1987, the C/D aircraft in today's fleet are much

RECONNAISSANCE HORNETS

In the fall of 1982, the Navy authorized McDonnell Douglas to begin work on a reconnaissance version of the Hornet. Original plans called for a dedicated two-seat version with a pod similar to the TARPS pod later developed for use by the F-14. However, modifications proved costly, both in money and weight, and that plan was quickly abandoned.

What followed was a single-seat proposal, called the F/A-18(R), which used a removable camera pallet installed in place of the M61A1 gun in the Hornet's nose. The pallet was designed for easy installation and conversion back to a gun-armed Hornet in just a few hours. The pallet contained a Fairchild-Weston low-/medium-altitude KA-99 panoramic camera, and a Honeywell AA-5 infrared linescanner (IRLS). The KA-99's low-altitude sensor provided a 140-degree field of view (FOV) for overflights at altitudes of 200 to 3,000 feet. The medium-altitude sensor featured a 22-degree FOV at altitudes of 3,000 to 25,000 feet and could be steered over a 220 degree swath at ranges of up to five miles. The IRLS operated with either a wide or narrow mode and at altitudes of 200 to 25,000 feet, but required overflight.

The pallet was installed by removing the lower nose fairings and adding a hinged and slightly bulged hatch, which had two square oblique slots for the optics. F/A-18A BuNo. 160775 was modified to this configuration and first flew on 15 August 1984. A second F/A-18A was also modified, BuNo. 161214, after the first was turned over to NASA. While a viable option, the F/A-18(R) was never adopted. However, because the fate of the F/A-18 was still uncertain when the C/D models entered production, the nose sections were designed for easy eventual depot refit to the (R) configuration.

The next reconnaissance version studied was the RF-18D for use by the Marines. This proposal used an all-weather Loral UPD-4 side-looking high-resolution synthetic aperture radar mounted on a centerline pod. Images would be viewable in the aft cockpit and could also be data linked to ground stations in near real-time. This pod was successfully prototyped on an RF-4 in 1986, and deliveries were planned beginning in 1990. However, the program was canceled as part of the defense drawdown at the end of the Cold War.

The Marines were then told to adopt the Advanced Tactical Air Reconnaissance System (ATARS) being developed by

Once modified, the ATARS pallet can be easily installed in an F/A-18D. (U.S. Navy)

The upper aircraft is carrying the datalink pod (on the centerline) to be used in conjunction with ATARS. No datalink pods were available until after Operation Allied Force ended. (U.S. Navy)

the Air Force for its F-16s, which utilized a pallet-mounted system similar to that used in the F/A-18(R). Accordingly, McDonnell Douglas began wiring its D variants to accommodate the pods, beginning with Lot XIV, Block 36, in anticipation of this capability. These are designated as the F/A-18D(RC) and a total of 52 have been built.

Again, money proved short and the Air Force abandoned the ATARS program in the fall of 1993. The Marines assumed management of the ATARS program in early 1994 and continued work on the system, testing the concept by flying five demonstration flights. The unit was placed in a modified 330-gallon fuel tank and mounted on the centerline of BuNo. 163434. ATARS uses similar cameras as the F/A-18(R), but adds a digital data-link pod for near-real-time transfer. Moreover, ATARS can be used with the planned APG-73 RUG II upgrade to create reconnaissance strip maps and high resolution spot maps embedded with digital radar data. An initial LRIP contract was awarded on 5 May 1997, for four ATARS pallets to use for testing. On 27 February 1998, a contract was awarded for six ATARS pallets and four data link pods, plus funds for associated logistics. At present, planned procurement calls for 31 ATARS pallets and conversion kits, and 24 data link pods.

Although still in testing, two ATARS-capable aircraft and three ATARS pallets were deployed by the Marine Corps during the recent conflict in the Balkans. Assigned to VMFA(AW)-332, these Hornets flew more than 50 missions, most of which were combined with others, rather than dedicated to reconnaissance. The systems worked well during the deployment and ATARS was recently approved for full-rate production, having completed its successful OPEVAL in April 2000. Currently on contract are 14 LRIP models, ten of which have already been delivered to the Marines. The full rate production will add five more systems, bringing the total to 19.

The F/A-18E/F Super Hornet will also feature a reconnaissance capability through the Shared Reconnaissance Pod (SHARP) program. SHARP replaces the F-14 TARPS and SHARP provides a greater standoff ability, permitting photography from a distance of up to 45 miles. Using Commercial-Off-the-Shelf (COTS), Non-Developmental Items (NDI), SHARP will enter the prototype phase in FY01 and should be available for the first projected F/A-18F cruise in 2002. One advantage of SHARP is that it is pod-mounted, thereby allowing retention of the gun, and also permitting more flexible adaptation as to which aircraft carries the pod.

improved from their predecessors. Again, this is reflective of the design flexibility and growth capacity of the original platform.

Several upgrades have followed to the Hornet's mission computer, the XN-6. Introduced in the C/D model, the XN-6 brought three-fold increase in processing capacity to the Hornet. This was soon replaced by the XN-8, and finally the XN-10. Other important changes saw the introduction of improved engines, the F404-GE-402 Enhanced Performance Engine (EPE). This engine, which produces 17,600 lb. thrust in afterburner, was designed at the request of the Kuwaitis and Swiss, who sought

more power for their Hornets. The Navy was so impressed with the uprated engines that it adopted them for U.S. models, beginning with Block 36 in January of 1991. The EPE engines offer even more thrust than meets the eye by a plain comparison of its numbers versus the F404-GE-400s. Certain portions of the flight regime are impacted more than others, such that an F/A-18C with EPEs performs 27 percent better than a non-EPE Hornet in transonic acceleration at 35,000 feet.

Lot XIII Hornets and beyond also saw the addition of an on-board oxygen generating system (OBOGS) in replace of the previous liquid

oxygen (LOX) converter system. Other enhancements include replacement in 1991 of the ASN-139 inertial navigation system (INS) with the ASN-39 laser-ring-gyro (LRG) system, the incorporation of a P-Code GPS receiver in 1995, and the radar upgrade known as APG-73. The APG-73 offers a better raid assessment mode, higher-resolution ground mapping modes, increased detection and tracking ranges (between 7 and 20 percent), and a better ability, through use of a wider bandwidth, to defeat enemy jamming.

Finally, a recent modification has seen the standard APX-100 IFF

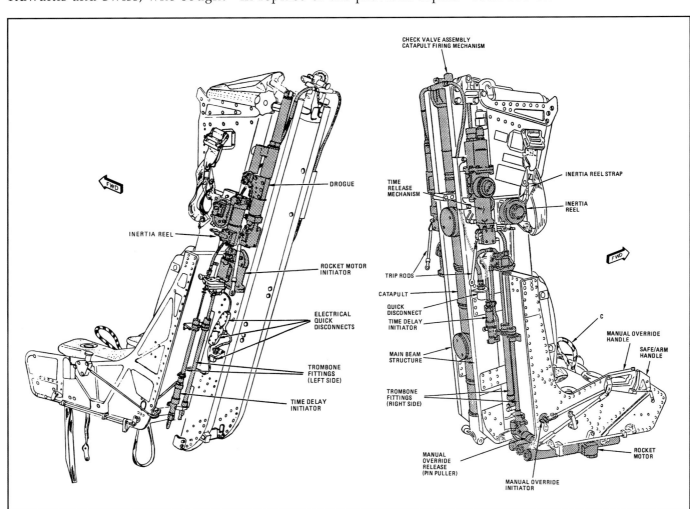

Two views of the Martin-Baker SJU-17/A ejection seat used by F/A-18Cs are shown here. (F/A-18 NATOPS)

This cluster of small stub antennas is for the ALR-67 reprogrammable radar warning receiver. The small blister houses the ALQ-126/165 antennas. The ALR-67 uses a sorting algorithms receiver to compare the perceived signals against those stored in its data banks, then provides a digital frequency readout and traditional display symbology showing the relative bearing of the threat versus the aircraft. The RWR uses four antennas, one on each side of the nose fuselage near the running lights and one on top of each vertical stabilizer, and a small array of five stub antennas under the gun door.
(John Binford)

(Identification Friend or Foe) replaced with an improved Hazeltine APX-113 Combined Interrogator Transponder (CIT). This is identifiable by a row of five short-blade antennas above the fighter's nose. The APX-113 features electronic beam steering that allows Hornet pilots to determine the range, bearing, and elevation of the interrogated aircraft. Kuwait was the first customer to use this IFF and installation in U.S. Hornets followed beginning in 1997. C/D Hornets were also the first to receive an AIM-120 AMRAAM capability, which enhanced their performance as fighters.

The two fairings behind the cockpit of this VFA-147 Argonaut F/A-18C are for the ALQ-165 self-protection jammer. Although the ALQ-165 was canceled, some 96 units were produced and placed in storage. Beginning with operations over Bosnia, the jammers have been installed on an "as needed" basis to forward-deployed squadrons. The small antenna is for TACAN; the larger, swept UHF/IFF antenna was installed on Lot 14 F/A-18C/Ds. Notice the freshly applied anti-skid surface around the spine and cockpit. (Brad Elward)

The AAS-38 Lockheed Martin (Loral) NITE Hawk FLIR is carried on left fuselage station and provides real-time thermal imaging. The FLIR uses a narrow (3 degree) and wide (12 degree) FOV and data obtained from it can be integrated with other Hornet sensors to help calculate weapons release solutions. The AAS-38A was used by VMFA(AW)-121 during Operation Desert Storm, although only four pods were available. Introduced to the fleet in January 1993, the AAS-38A, offered the ability to designate targets for laser-guided munitions. Designated as the laser target designator/ranger (LTD/R), the AAS-38A is also called a targeting FLIR or T-FLIR. A laser spot tracker was added with the AAS-38B. During the Super Hornet's EMD and OpEval, a modified version of the AAS-38 (the AAS-46) was used to test T-FLIR functionality. (Ted Carlson)

The F/A-18C/D vertical tails have an additional fairing from their A/B predecessor. The starboard tail, at forefront, features a position light (top), ALR-67 tail warning antenna (middle), and a fairing for the ALQ-165 low-band transmitter. (Brad Elward)

Shown here is the tailhook and a close view of the two F404-GE-400 engines. The Enhanced Performance Engine F402 has a white interior and is made of ceramics. (Brad Elward)

An F402-GE-400 sits on a cart at NAS Oceana. This engine may be used for either bay, and can be easily installed by sliding the pallet under the fuselage and raising the engine into position. (Brad Elward)

F/A-18 HORNET WEAPONS

Given its dual mission role, the Hornet occupies the rare position of being one of the few aircraft cleared for virtually all weapons in the Navy's arsenal. The Hornet's sole organic weapon is its internal M61A1 20-mm six-barrel cannon. Made by GE, the M61A1 has a 578-round capacity and can fire at rates of 4,000 or 6,000 rounds per minute at velocities in excess of 3,400 feet per second. The Hornet also has nine weapons stations, two of which are located on the fuselage. Wingtip stations, designated as 1 and 9 from left to right, can carrying the AIM-9 Sidewinder and instrumentation pods for ACM. There are two stations on each wing, each rated at 2,600 lbs. The inboard stations (and the centerline station) are plumbed for external fuel tanks. The wing stations can be fitted with multiple (dual) and triple ejection racks, although the latter are not cleared for carrier operations.

Controlling the Hornet's weapons arsenal is the Smiths Industries AYQ-9(V) weapons control and stores management system. The AYQ-9(V) can control and monitor 50 types of weapons and 11 types of naval mines, providing air crews with information on weapons operational readiness and automatically establishing sequencing.

The principal air-to-air weapons of the Hornet are the infrared-seeking AIM-9 Sidewinder, and the radar-guided AIM-7 Sparrow and AIM-120 AMRAAM. The current Sidewinder variant is the AIM-9M, which features an all-aspect capability, as well as enhanced counter-countermeasure systems. By using MERs, a Hornet can carry as many as eight AIM-9s. The AIM-7 was intended as the Hornet's primary air-to-air weapon, but has since been replaced by the more capable fire-and-forget AIM-120. Indeed, one of the principal drawbacks to the AIM-7 was the need for the pilot to maintain a radar lock through the entire flight envelope, which in turn required the pilot to fly a relatively straight and predictable flightpath.

The Hornet's air-to-ground arsenal has changed over the years from one of unguided iron bombs to that of a sophisticated mix of precision-guided weapons. The Mk 80 series iron bombs are the Hornet's most basic weapon and come in weights of 500

The AGM-62 Walleye is seen on this Marine Corps VFMA(AW)-533 at Twentynine Palms in 1994. (Ted Carlson)

This VFA-192 Hornet is seen during the opening days of Operation Desert Storm with four AGM-88 HARMs. The fake canopy painted on the underside is a trick used by most U.S. Marine Corps squadrons and all Canadian Hornets. (LT Eric Meyer, USN via National Naval Aviation Museum)

(Mk 82), 1,000 (Mk 83), and 2,000 (Mk 84) pounds. These can be equipped with conical fins or retarders (snake eyes). A special hardened target variant is also produced called the BLU-109. Dumb weaponry also include cluster munitions: CBU-59/B Rockeye; CBU-78/B Gator (antitank); and CBU-87B combined effect munitions (CEM).

Guided missiles are also in the Hornet's weaponry. Two of the more common are the AGM-62 Walleye and AGM-65 Maverick. The Walleye is really a glide bomb and is intended for larger targets such as fuel tanks and bridges. Two variants have been used, the Walleye I, which uses a tone data link, and the Walleye II, which uses a differential-phase-shift-keyed digital data link and requires guidance from an AWW-9B data link pod via video imagery. Maverick is a rocket-propelled missile that is for use against tanks and other vehicles. The Navy uses the AGM-65E and F variants, which utilize a laser and infrared seeker respectively.

The Hornet can also launch members of the AGM-84 family, including the AGM-84D Harpoon, the AGM-84E SLAM, and the new AGM-84H SLAM-ER (expanded range). The Harpoon is an antiship missile with a range of approximately 70 nms and relies on active radar seeker for target tracking. SLAM is essentially the Harpoon missile mated with the Maverick's infrared guidance unit and the Walleye's INS/GPS navigation unit and data link. SLAM and the SLAM-ER may be used against shore-based facilities and up to four of the AGM-84 missiles can be carried on the wing stations using the AERO-65 or AERO-7/A bomb racks.

During the 1980s, Hornet's carried the AGM-45 Shrike anti-radiation missile, but today, the premiere radar-killer is the AGM-88 High-speed Anti-Radiation Missile (HARM), of which four can be carried on the wing stations. The HARM uses terminal homing and possesses a fire-and-forget capability. The latest version used is the AGM-88C Block V, which features a "home-on-jam" capability and an enhanced capability to remember a target's location should the emitter be turned off. HARMs are carried for the SEAD mission and can be turned on while still mounted to provide better detection and location.

The J-series weapons are the latest in the Hornet's arsenal. JSOW, the Joint Stand-off Weapon is a glide weapon that can be launched from distances of up to 46 miles at high altitude

Dual Zuni rocket pods can be carried on MERs, for a total of eight. (Rick Morgan)

An excellent view of the AIM-7F and AIM-9L air-to-air missiles. The Hornet is an F/A-18A from VFA-25 during 1984. (Rick Morgan)

released and carries one of three warhead types. The Baseline JSOW (AGM-154A) carries 145 BLU-97A/B combined effects bomblets (CEBs) for soft targets and vehicles. AGM-154B features six BLU-108/B sensor-fused submunitions and is for anti-armor. JSOW A/B rely on a GPS/INS system for midcourse navigation and use imaging infrared (IIR) for terminal homing. The final variant, AGM-154C, is exclusively

for Navy use and is to replace the Walleye. It will use a combination of an IIR terminal seeker and AAW-9B or AAW-13 data link for guidance. JSOW was delivered for fleet use beginning in June 1998 and VFA-81 became the first Hornet squadron certified to carry the weapon.

The newly-developed Joint Direct Attack Munitions (JDAM) is designated GBU-29/30/31/32 and is

essentially an Mk 80 series bomb integrated with a GPS/INS guidance kit. JDAM modifies the bombs by adding a new tail kit and costs just $18,000 per kit. Boeing makes the JDAM in four sizes corresponding to the Mk 80 series and beginning with the 250 lb. Mk 81. With demonstrated accuracy of as little as 40 feet, JDAM has established itself as the poor man's precision weapon. The AGM-158 Joint Air-to-Surface Stand-off Missile (JASSM) is produced by Lockheed Martin and will enter fleet service in 2001. It has a 1,000-lb. unitary warhead and a range of up to 100 nm. Guidance is provided by GPS/INS, with IIR terminal guidance and a pattern-matching autonomous target recognition system. JASSM will only be carried by the E/F Super Hornet.

Since the Gulf War, efforts have succeeded developing a highly-capable laser-guided capability for the Hornet. F/A-18C/Ds are now equipped with the AAS-38B designator and will in the future receive the vastly superior ATFLIR, which will provide better infrared resolution and range, as well as an improved autonomous laser. LGBs are a kit added to Mk 80 series bombs. Hornets typically carry three classes of LGBs: the GBU-12, based on the 500-lb. Mk 82; GBU-16, based on the 1,000-lb. Mk 83; and GBU-10, based on the 2,000-lb. Mk 84. A special version, GBU-24, is also used for hardened targets, and is based on the 2,000-lb. BLU-109/B.

Other munitions include: 2.75-inch and 5-inch folding-fin rockets, a variety of mines, and B57 and B61 nuclear weapons. ADM-141 tactical air-launched decoys (TALDs) and miniature air-launched decoys (MALDs) can also be carried. These devices emit electronic signals to simulate the

signature of a fighter or bomber, thereby drawing fire or radar paints from enemy air defenses. TALDs were used frequently in the Persian Gulf War during attacks against Baghdad. The TALD is a glide decoy while the MALD has a 50-lb. thrust Sundstrand TJ-50 turbojet.

Two Mk 82 500-lb. bombs are on this Canted Vertical Ejection Rack (CVER). F/A-18s originally carried the vertical ejection rack (VER), but later converted to a "canted" rack to improve bomb clearance during multiple release. The CVER may carry up to two Mk 83 (1,000-lb)-class stores, and is used solely by the F/A-18. (Boeing)

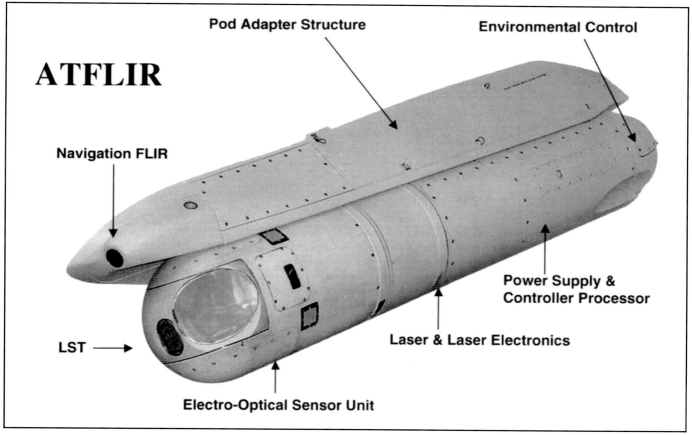

ATFLIR

- Pod Adapter Structure
- Environmental Control
- Navigation FLIR
- Power Supply & Controller Processor
- LST →
- Laser & Laser Electronics
- Electro-Optical Sensor Unit

Future Hornets (both the E/F and some C/D) will carry Raytheon's ATFLIR navigation and infrared targeting pod. ATFLIR incorporates third generation mid-wave infrared (MWIR) staring focal plane technology, and has substantially greater recognition and laser designation range as compared to current Navy FLIRs. The system made its first flight in November 1999 and has been recently approved for LRIP. IOC is planned for 2002, although efforts are being made to ready it for the first Super Hornet cruise in 2001. ATFLIR should prove superior to the F-14 LANTIRN system and make the Hornet the weapon of choice for night attack. (Raytheon)

A VFA-82 shown in the self-escort configuration with four Mk 83 1,000-lb. bombs, two AIM-7s, and two AIM-9s, plus a centerline fuel tank. This is a Pre-Lot XIV F/A-18C, as evidenced by the smaller and vertical UHF/IFF antenna of the upper fuselage. (Boeing)

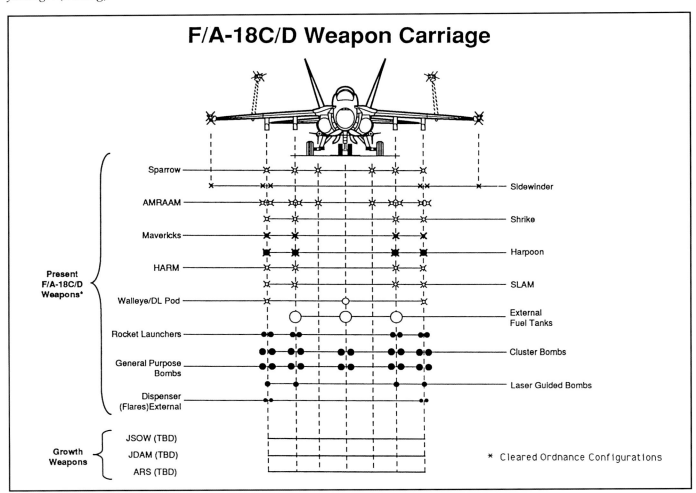

Current and projected weapons that can be carried by the F/A-18C/D. (F/A-18 NATOPS)

Three F/A-18Ds of Marine Air Group (MAG) 11 from (front-to-back) VMFA(AW)-121, -225, -242. The Marines Corps is the only U.S. service to operate the two-place in a tactical role and has done so marvelously. Marine Ds fly FAC missions, and use the new ATARS reconnaissance pod to provide battlefield reconnaissance. (Robert Lawson via National Naval Aviation Museum)

Several F/A-18s undergo an overhaul at the Naval Aviation Depot Facility. The Hornet in the forefront is from VFA-86 Sidewinders, followed by one from VFA-83 Rampagers, and VFA-113 Stingers. (Rick Burgess)

These three photos show the Hornet driver's "office." Clearly visible are the three box-shaped displays and the left side dual throttles. The hook-lowering handle is on the right of the instrument panel; the landing gear controls are at the far left, just below the yellow and black "handle."
(Brad Elward)

The D has been successful overseas as evidenced by the Malaysian procurement of eight F/A-18Ds in 1997. This D is painted in the same gunship gray color scheme as the F-15E Strike Eagle. (Boeing)

Hornets flying over Bosnia and the No-fly zones of Iraq often fly with mixed (flex) loads that permit pilots to perform a variety of missions. This Marine Corps Hornet carries a Maverick missile, FLIR, LGB, and Mk 82 bomb for air-to-ground missions and two AIM-9s and a single AIM-7 for air defense. Two external tanks are also shown. (Boeing)

This laser-guided bomb, seen on the middle wing pylon, awaits a test flight at NAS Patuxent River during 1997. The added pylon permits a more flexible payload and ultimately means fewer aircraft are needed on any particular strike. (Boeing)

A "lex fence" was added to Hornets beginning in March 1988 to alter the air flow over the vertical tail fins and reduce vibrations that were inducing cracks. (Ted Carlson)

Illustrated here are the hand-controllers used by F/A-18D WSOs to control sensors and weapons. (F/A-18D NATOPS)

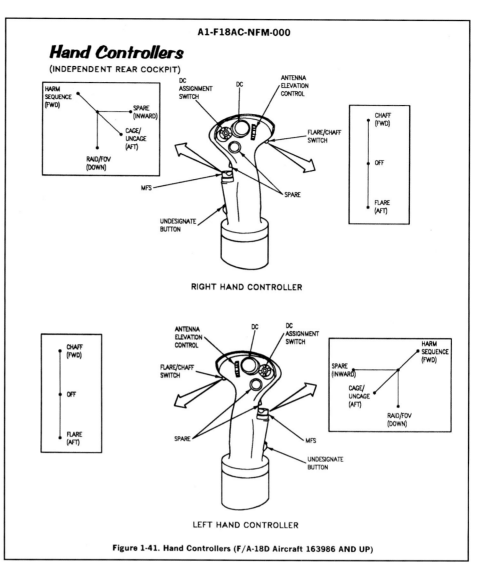

Hand Controllers
(INDEPENDENT REAR COCKPIT)

RIGHT HAND CONTROLLER

LEFT HAND CONTROLLER

Figure 1-41. Hand Controllers (F/A-18D Aircraft 163986 AND UP)

The AAR-50 Thermal Imaging Navigation Set (TINS) was introduced with the Night Attack Hornets for night navigation and is mounted on the right fuselage station. It features a 19.5-degree FOV, which is presented as raster video on the HUD. Interim clearance was given during the fall of 1990 for VMFA(AW)-121 to begin training with the pod in anticipation of the pending conflict in the Persian Gulf. AAR-50 was cleared for fleet use in October 1992. (Bill Kistler)

AGM-65 Mavericks are outstanding weapons for use against vehicles and tanks. Shown here is the AGM-65E laser-guided version, but the Hornet may also carry the AGM-65F imaging infrared-guided version. (Boeing)

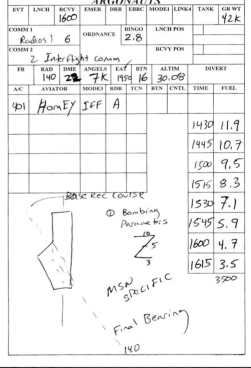

The addition of the second crew member in the F/A-18D enhances the F/A-18's tactical flexibility and allows crews to perform FAC missions, and also operate more efficiently in high-threat areas and in bad weather or night low-level flights. Shown here are Captains B.J. "Fuego" Nownes and William "Bouncer" Bensch of VMFA(AW)-121. (Ted Carlson)

A typical kneeboard card carried by Hornet pilots outlines some of the information the pilot might need during the mission. The pilot has sketched his bombing parameters, base recovery course, and fuel ladder on this card. (Brad Elward)

A NEW BEGINNING

HORNET 2000 AND THE BIRTH OF THE E/F

During the 1980s, aircraft carrier decks were filled with a variety of single-mission aircraft. Fleet defense was provided by the F-14, while the close-in fighter role was filled by the F/A-18A. Light attack was handled by the A-7 and the F/A-18A, although the former was being slowly phased out. Medium and all-weather attack was handled by the Vietnam-vintage A-6E and reconnaissance was provided by a combination of RF-8 and F-14 with TARPS pods. Because these aircraft were at the end of their growth capabilities, several programs were begun to develop follow-on platforms.

Two of these programs represented the high-end of the technological spectrum and were recognized as extremely costly. The Naval Advanced Tactical Fighter (NATF), essentially a navalized F-22, was planned as the replacement for the F-14, the Navy's preeminent fleet defense fighter and interceptor. The super-stealthy flying wing A-12 Avenger II was slated to replace the A-6 medium bomber. While each of these aircraft did meet the growing Soviet threat and would do so for years to come, both were still many years away from fleet introduction. As a result, the Navy needed a stop-gap capability to carry the fleet until these new high-end aircraft became operational. Thus, in July 1987, the Department of Defense issued directives to the Navy and the Air Force to explore derivatives of the F/A-18 and the F-16 to fill the gap until the F-22 and the A-12 arrived in the early part of the 21st Century.

McDonnell Douglas' response to this call was the Hornet 2000 program.

HORNET 2000

Begun in late 1987, Hornet 2000 studies evaluated a wide range of concepts in an effort to determine how to continue the F/A-18's evolution. Several concepts were reviewed, ranging from modifying the FY88 baseline aircraft with improved avionics and survivability packages, uprated engines, and a raised dorsal spine with more fuel, to a full-blown redesign called the Hornet 2000 Configuration IV. Intermediate designs featured combinations of a raised dorsal section, a fuselage plug, and larger or stiffened wings. Configuration IV featured a delta-shaped wing with small canards and closely resembled the Dassault-Breguet Rafaele. Each of the Hornet 2000 alternatives offered distinct

trade-offs in capabilities, but all had the common theme of redressing identified deficiencies of the baseline F/A-18. Not only were these designs made available to the U.S. Navy, but foreign buyers were courted as well. McDonnell Douglas actively marketed the Hornet 2000 design to several countries, including West Germany, and France, as a competitor in what became known as the Eurofighter 2000 program. Despite great efforts, McDonnell Douglas was unable to generate any interest and the program was shelved.

COLD WAR RESTRUCTURING ALTERS PLANS

The end of the Cold War and the demise of the Soviet Union in 1988 signaled a dramatic change in naval aviation procurement. Wars of the future would no longer be fought in the open seas against Soviet long-

This F/A-18E cutaway shows the extended fuselage fuel tanks and the additional weapons stations on the wings. Notice the four boxes in the LEX aft of the retracted ladder. (Boeing)

A wind-tunnel model of the F/A-18E seen in June 1993. (Boeing)

range bombers and vast fleets of missile-carrying ships and submarines, but rather in the littoral regions – those areas within a few hundred miles from the shore lines. This realization brought with it a fundamental change in war-fighting tactics and further demanded a reexamination of the weapons needed to fight such wars.

As a result of this change in thought, many perceived no need for the weapons that fought the Cold War

of yesteryear. This view, coupled with severe program cost overruns and schedule slips, led to the cancellation of the A-12 aircraft in January 1991. Only a few years before, in partial anticipation of the A-12, Congress had terminated the A-6F Intruder II upgrade and it had only recently scaled back procurement of the improved F-14D to just 54 aircraft. These events left naval aviation with only the A-X, the Navy's planned replacement for the A-6E, the Hornet 2000 proposal (ultimately the F/A-18E/F), and a ground-attack modified F-14X. When the NATF program was terminated due to the inappropriateness of a navalized F-22, the A-X program was restructured to become AF-X with a dual role requirement and with Air Force participation. This program saw rapidly escalating requirements and unconstrained cost growth resulting in its ultimate cancellation. When the AFX program was canceled and the F-14X proposal rejected, only the E/F strike-fighter remained for the Navy.

Other events also occurred during the early 1990s that shaped the future of the new Hornet. In 1993, the military underwent its first major restructuring since the end of the Cold War. Called the Bottom Up Review (BUR), the conclusion was simply that the U.S. could not afford all of the defense programs that evolved out of the 1980s. Thus, the Air Force chose to push its F-22 air superiority fighter and the Navy stood behind the E/F. The BUR also ended the A/F-X and the intended F-16 replacement, the Multi-Role Fighter (MRF), on the ground that they were unaffordable. These were replaced with the Joint Affordable Strike technology (JAST) program which eventually evolved into a light multi-mission aircraft called the Joint

A 1993 computer rendition of the F/A-18E depicts the Super Hornet carrying a variety of stores, including Sidewinders, AMRAAMs, T/FLIR, two AGM-84E SLAMs, and an AWW-13 data link pod. (Boeing)

Strike Fighter (JSF). This move meant the Air Force would operate a combination of F-22 and the JSF, while the Navy and the Marines would operate the F/A-18E/F and JSF.

One facet of the Super Hornet's development that is often misunderstood is the fiscal background of the early 1990s against which the decision to acquire the E/F was made. During the early 1990s, defense funds were dwindling and there was a strong movement to curb defense spending even further. This put the Navy in a rather harsh predicament, as it was faced with an aging fleet of aircraft. Moreover, most of its follow-on designs had been canceled and labeled as too costly in the post-Cold War world. Because of cost concerns, the Navy quickly realized that the cost factor, more than any other, would shape future naval aircraft.

The Navy's decision to develop the E/F over various strike-configured F-14 proposals met with considerable opposition from many in the media and the Tomcat community. Proponents of a strike-capable F-14D argued that the Tomcat offered superior speed, greater range and payload, and could carry the long-ranged AIM-54C Phoenix air-to-air missile, which the Super Hornet could not.

F/A-18E/F supporters discounted the radar advantage, given the high level of integration of today's air wing, as all information can be gathered by the carrier's E-2C Hawkeye surveillance aircraft and relevant information passed to airborne fleet units. This is now being realized through the multi-function information distribution system (MIDS), which performs the same function that the long-canceled F/A-18C JTDS program was supposed to pro-

vide. Supporters also responded that F-14D's superior speed is less important and is offset by the Super Hornet's better handling qualities and that the Phoenix capability was no longer needed for fleet defense given the demise of the Soviet Union and its massive fleets of long-ranged bombers.

Other issues also impacted the Navy's decision, namely the high cost of maintaining the F-14 and the fact that the E/F presented a new and modern design. A rivalry (not always friendly) existed between the Tomcat and Hornet communities for several years, but as former F-14 air crew began to play an important role in the design and development of the dual-seat F/A-18F, and the Tomcat developed its own strike capability, this has evolved into a cooperative relationship, with Tomcat crews in the forefront of those transitioning into the Super Hornet.

SUPER HORNET CONCEPTS

Vice Admiral Joseph Dyer, Commander, Naval Air Systems Command and former F/A-18 Program Manager from 1994 through 1997, has explained how the Hornet 2000 program and a major shift in thinking during the late 1980s impacted on what became the Super Hornet. "There was a recognition in the late 1980s that we simply could not do things the same way in procurement." There was also a recognition that the Navy needed to replace a certain number of aircraft within a particular price, Dyer added. Dyer credits two individuals, Pam O'Dell of NAVAIR and Darryl Davis, a McDonnell Douglas engineer, with changing the focus of the Hornet 2000 program. "They looked at how much money was available at the time and at how many aircraft were needed to do the job the Navy needed done. This allowed us to fix a number, then work

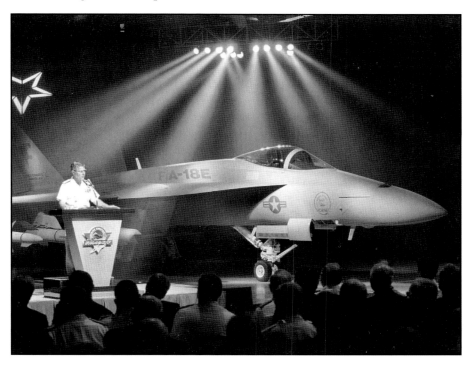

F/A-18E was rolled out at Boeing's St. Louis, Missouri facility on 18 September 1995. Admiral Jeremy Boorda, former Chief of Naval Operations, spoke at that event and named the F/A-18E/F the Super Hornet. (Boeing)

to develop a design that fell within it. Building a plane that costs $150 million per copy with a $50 billion cost of development was simply out of the question."

Dyer also acknowledged that there had been a move away from the old concept of developing a "stand-alone" aircraft to what he termed as "systems thinking" whereby aircraft rely on other assets – tankers, jammers, escort – to accomplish the task at hand. "We used to look at a design in isolation," Dyer said, "without reference to the systems at large. In doing that, we took affordability out of the picture. With Hornet 2000, we sought to bring that issue back to the table to meet the Navy's needs." In fact, what Dyer is referencing by "systems thinking" can be seen not only by looking to the interaction between the E-2C and the planes it controls, but also to the ways Operations Desert Storm, Desert Fox, and Allied Force were fought using "composite" forces (or systems) coordinated through joint air tasking

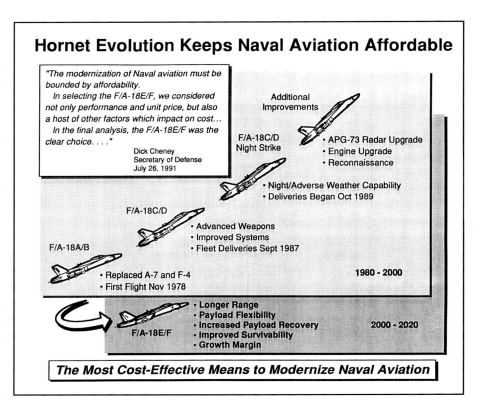

Hornet Evolution Keeps Naval Aviation Affordable

"The modernization of Naval aviation must be bounded by affordability.
    In selecting the F/A-18E/F, we considered not only performance and unit price, but also a host of other factors which impact on cost...
    In the final analysis, the F/A-18E/F was the clear choice. . . ."

Dick Cheney
Secretary of Defense
July 26, 1991

Additional Improvements
• APG-73 Radar Upgrade
• Engine Upgrade
• Reconnaissance

F/A-18C/D Night Strike
• Night/Adverse Weather Capability
• Deliveries Began Oct 1989

F/A-18C/D
• Advanced Weapons
• Improved Systems
• Fleet Deliveries Sept 1987

F/A-18A/B
• Replaced A-7 and F-4
• First Flight Nov 1978

1980 - 2000

F/A-18E/F
• Longer Range
• Payload Flexibility
• Increased Payload Recovery
• Improved Survivability
• Growth Margin

2000 - 2020

The Most Cost-Effective Means to Modernize Naval Aviation

This Boeing chart shows the Hornet's evolution and the development of the E/F, which basically restarted the "growth clock" for the aircraft. (Boeing)

orders (ATOs). Navy aircraft flew in concert with Air Force assets as well as those of our NATO allies. Air wars today are not fought in isolation, but require well-coordinated groups of aircraft. Fighters and attack aircraft rely on tankers, suppression of enemy air defenses (SEAD), escort, and radar control aircraft in high threat areas; even the F-117 flies with electronic warfare escorts.

The merging of these concepts created more receptive attitude towards trade-offs. "We asked ourselves, 'how much stealth is enough?'" Dyer answered his rhetorical question, "Enough to deliver stand-off weapons, such as JSOW, with excellent survivability." He then provided an example of this, noting that there are several ways to reduce observability, just as there are several ways to increase an aircraft's ability to get its nose on a target to obtain a firing solution. Survivability can be achieved through designs such as those used on the F-117, B-2, and

Before carrier qualifications, the F/A-18E had to be tested at a ground station to ensure that it could withstand the rigors of a carrier launch. (Boeing)

F-22, which rely primarily on stealth, but at considerable procurement and life cycle support costs. On the other hand, low-survivability can be achieved by using radar-absorbing materials, electronics, and innovative use of stand-off weapons and tactics. One of the problems in placing too much emphasis on any one factor is the risk of an adversary developing counter tactics. The recent shoot down of an F-117 during Operation Allied Force only illustrates this point. "The key is finding the right balance, within the confines of affordability."

Cluster bombs like this Mk 20 Rockeye were one of the 29 weapons configurations presented for review during the F/A-18E/F OPEVAL. (Boeing)

Certainly the Super Hornet represents a compromise of several characteristics, but these compromises nevertheless resulted in a phenomenal aircraft. Dyer adds, "The Super Hornet is best thought of as the 'sports utility vehicle' of Navy TacAir. Because of what we sought to design – the premier strike-fighter – the aircraft can be criticized on either of the extremes: It is not a high-speed interceptor, and it is not a bomb truck." Total success at either extreme requires a dedicated platform design – one tailored to the specific mission. Necessarily, these "end-spectrum" designs are not mutually supportable to each missions needs. "But the E/F," Dyer continued, "stakes out the middle of the spectrum and its design allows it to expand out left and right as far out as possible," thereby providing battlegroup commanders with the most flexible platform possible for conducting offensive air operations. Again, we come back to ask, "What is the threat and how can we best meet that threat in an affordable way?"

THE SUPER HORNET EMERGES

The F/A-18E/F represented the middle-road configuration of the 11 Hornet 2000 designs, combining a stretched fuselage with an enlarged wing and various avionics improvements. The Navy quickly supported this measure and pressed for its approval in late 1991. The program initially suffered from the same cost and weight overruns experienced by the A-12. A major refocus, however, brought matters back in line and the program has been a model of efficiency and affordability ever since. Congressional approval and a $4.88 billion (in FY92 dollars) engineering and manufacturing development (EMD) contract followed on 17 July 1992. On 7 December 1992, the Navy

The sixth F/A-18E during assembly on 28 May 1998. Note the large pivot points for the horizontal stabilizer protruding from the aft fuselage below the rudder. The lighter areas are metal (usually aluminum) alloy covered in a zinc coating, while the dark skin is composite. (Boeing)

signed the definitized F/A-18E/F development contract, calling for three ground test airframes (ST-50 for static loads; DT-50 for drop, barricade, and live fire testing; and FT-50 for fatigue loads), five single-seat F/A-18Es, and two F/A-18Fs. As with the Hornet, the E/F was to be produced in partnership by McDonnell Douglas and Northrop Grumman.

Production of the center/aft fuselage for E1 (BuNo. 165164) began in May 1994 at Northrop Grumman's El Segundo California facility and the assembly line opened in St. Louis on 23 September. E1 was rolled out from the St. Louis facility on 18 September 1995 where it was named the Super Hornet and took to the air on 29 November with McDonnell Douglas test pilot Fred

Madenwald at the controls. E1 was flown to Patuxent River, Maryland, on 15 February 1996 to begin its flight tests.

INITIAL PROCUREMENT

The initial F/A-18E/F procurement contract entered into during March 1997 was separated into three lots calling for 62 total aircraft to be delivered in batches of 12 (LRIP 1 in FY 97), 20 (LRIP 2 in FY 98), and 30 (LRIP 3 in FY 99). LRIP-1 aircraft (8 Es and 4 Fs) were all delivered ahead of schedule (the last by 9 November 1999). LRIP-2 aircraft were delivered between January and October 2000, and LRIP-3 deliveries commenced in November 2000, with final deliveries slated for July 2001.

Early LRIP aircraft were used for the Operational Evaluation, began in May 1999, and to stock the new FRS, VFA-122, and the first Super Hornet squadron, VFA-115. Full-rate production of 36 Super Hornets (15 Es and 21 Fs) began in 2000, and 42 (14 Es and 28 Fs) are scheduled for 2001. Current plans are for 548 Super Hornets, although this number could change depending on the status and availability of the JSF, future Marine Corps needs, and the outcome of the EA-6B follow-on studies.

Many defense analysts predict larger sales, including foreign military sales. Several allied nations are going to need new tactical aircraft before the Joint Strike Fighter is available and the Super Hornet possesses many attributes not inherent in the Eurofighter or the Rafaele. Moreover, avionics and subsystem commonality with the relatively large fleets of early model Hornets around the world make the choice to upgrade to the E/F affordable and appealing.

When seen together, the size difference between the F/A-18C (background) and F/A-18E (foreground) is obvious. The E is 2.83 feet longer, with 25 percent more wing area, and 40 percent greater range. The Super Hornet's larger stabilators are also prominent. (Boeing)

HORNET'S NEST

COLORFUL HORNETS IN SERVICE

When the F/A-18 Hornet was introduced to fleet service in the 1980s, it was long after the heyday of colorful squadron markings. Presently, most U.S. Navy and Marine Corps squadrons appear in a two-tone or three-tone gray scheme with muted black or gray markings. Exceptions to the two-tone color rule are seen in prototypes, EMD aircraft, and a few special squadrons. Originally, the F/A-18s were painted, from lightest to darkest, FS 36495 Light Gray (underside) with FS 36375 Light Ghost Gray (middle fuselage and top). FS 35237 Dark Blue Gray was then used for the anti-glare panel just ahead of the cockpit. These have subsequently been changed to FS 36375 Light Compass Gray for the underside, and FS 36320 Dark Compass Gray for the sides and top, with FS 35237 remaining the anti-glare coating.

Special purpose squadrons, such as the adversary aircraft of VFC-12 and -13, as well as those of VFA-127, had donned camouflage markings in an attempt to simulate threat aircraft commonly seen in the Middle East and Russia. VFC-12's Fighting Omars, for example, sport a colorful two-tone blue camouflage similar to that worn by Russian Su-27 aircraft.

Today, only the CAG birds, recognizable by their X00 modex, display any color, although that is usually relegated to the tail markings. The black-tailed CAG-birds of CVW-14 are well-known for their colorful and festive markings.

Some of the most colorful Hornets in the world are found in Canada's armed forces. Here, a CF-188A (BuNo. 188718) from 410 Squadron is seen at CFB Comox, BC in July 1999. (Mark Munzel)

Flying with a flex load, this Hornet is ready for most missions. Two AIM-9s and at least one AIM-120 are carried, plus one AGM-65 Maverick, and two CBU cluster bombs. A single Mk-83 iron bomb appears to be on the centerline station. (CPL Tomas Villanuevanr, USMC)

This pilot wears anti-scratch boots while walking on skin surfaces. The starboard wing holds a HARM, SLAM-ER, and JSOW from outboard in. (Boeing)

A sharp view of the unveiled Super Hornet in September 1995. (Boeing)

VFA-122 was officially established as the F/A-18E/F FRS at NAS Lemoore in January 1998. This F/A-18F sits on the ramp awaiting its student and instructor. (Ted Carlson)

VFA-37's Bulls are assigned to CVW-3 and presently fly F/A-18Cs. This Bull is dressed for the CAG, in partial high-visibility colors. (Mark Munzel)

F/A-18F1 catapults into history as the first Super Hornet to launch from a carrier. Piloted by CDR Tom Gurney, F1 climbs into foreboding skies off the coast of South Carolina. (Boeing)

The Super Hornet began appearing at airshows in 2000. Shown here at Andrews AFB during may 2000 is an F/A-18E/F (BuNo 165673) with VFA-122 markings and a smaple bo,mb load. (Mark Munzel)

Blue Angel No. 3 taxis on the tarmac. (Bill Kistler)

WARBIRDTECH
SERIES

With the introduction of the AAS-38B laser designator pod, Hornets could designate their own targets for LGB delivery. This opened an entirely new mission for the F/A-18, as they were no longer dependent on buddy lasing from other air wing A-6Es. (National Naval Aviation Museum)

The first Hornet undergoes preflight engine tests during early November 1995. The landing gear have been chocked and chained. (Boeing)

VFC-12's Fighting Omars are the sole remaining adversary squadron and are based at NAS Oceana, Virginia. The Omars are known for their Su-27-style two-tone blue camouflage and fly F/A-18As. (John Binford)

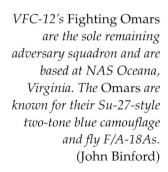

A colorful F/A-18B from NSAWC is seen over the Pacific Ocean.
(Ted Carlson)

NASA uses a small number of Hornets for test flights and for experimental testing on advanced aerodynamics. NASA has used F/A-18As like the one shown here for high AoA tests and modified Hornets for evaluating thrust-vectored technology. Note that the wing is missing.
(Mark Munzel)

VFA-115 transitioned to the F/A-18C from A-6E Intruders, but soon will fly the new Super Hornet. Shown here is the colorful CAG bird, BuNo. 163439.
(Mark Munzel)

This view from the simulator shows how the various screens actually appear to Hornet pilots during their missions. The pilot has a radar image displayed on the right MFD and has the infrared display from a FLIR on the left MFD and the HUD. Notice the digital readout for the fuel gauges at lower left. (Boeing)

BOEING
F/A-18 HORNET

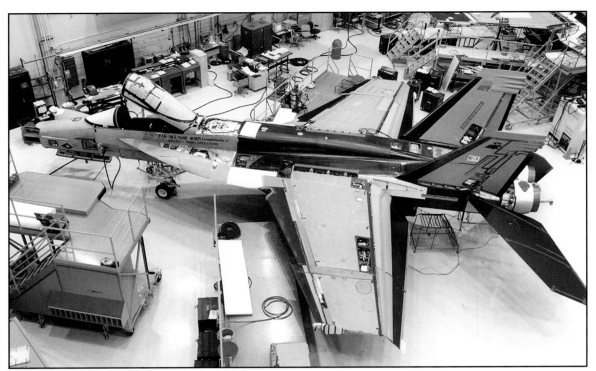

Shown in its black and flat green/yellow underskin, F/A-18E1, the first production Hornet, sits at St. Louis undergoing work. Many of the access panels have yet to be applied and several component areas are visible. (Boeing)

Removal of an engine is achieved by opening the engine bay from the bottom. (Boeing)

THE F/A-18E/F

TOMORROW'S HOPE FOR NAVAL AVIATION

Identifying any one factor as key to the Super Hornet's design is a difficult task, as most are inter-related and thus overlap to some degree. Certainly, designers sought to increase the aircraft's range over that of the C/D; yet, it was also stressed that the Hornet lacked sufficient bringback capability.

Rear Admiral James Godwin, III, currently Program Executive Officer, Tactical Aircraft Programs and a former F/A-18 Program Manager, believes that this factor was the key motivator of the F/A-18E/F: "People have to understand that it was this factor, the bringback capability, that really necessitated the Super Hornet coming into being." Bringback, says Godwin, means how much of an unused weapons load can be recovered back aboard the carrier after the mission has been flown. "This becomes extremely important," Godwin said, "with the high cost of precision weapons, and over regions such as the Persian Gulf and Bosnia where we are flying missions daily over the no-fly zones. To protect themselves against most contingencies,

The Super Hornet will form the backbone of American naval aviation for the next 25 years. The Super Hornet can perform all tactical missions presently covered by the Hornet, Tomcat, and Prowler, and can serve as an organic tanker and reconnaissance platform.
(Boeing)

Hornets flying over Southern Iraq often carry a mixed load of air-to-air and air-to-ground munitions. Our pilots have to be able to bring those unused weapons back aboard or we face jettisoning them into the waters of the Gulf." The E/F enables crews to return to the carrier with up to 9,000 lbs. of weapons/fuel, as compared to 5,500 lbs. with the late-model F/A-18C.

GROWTH IS A PRIME FACTOR

Another factor giving rise to the Super Hornet's birth was the limited growth potential of the C/D for new technologies. "The growth capacity built in to the original design was exhausted," Boeing's Paul Summers, F/A-18 Program New Products Manager, has explained. "What the E/F offered was the chance to 'set back the clock' and start at a full growth base." Room for growth has therefore been built-in to the Super Hornet airframe and systems such that new capabilities can be added over time without degrading the aircraft's performance. The Super Hornet will enter service with about 40 percent growth capacity in electrical power, air cooling, and equipment volume. The C/D has just 0.2 cubic feet of space remaining for future systems growth (about the size of a soda can); the E begins its operational career with 17.5 cubic feet.

The E/F represented the first airframe upgrade to the basic Hornet design; all prior modifications were

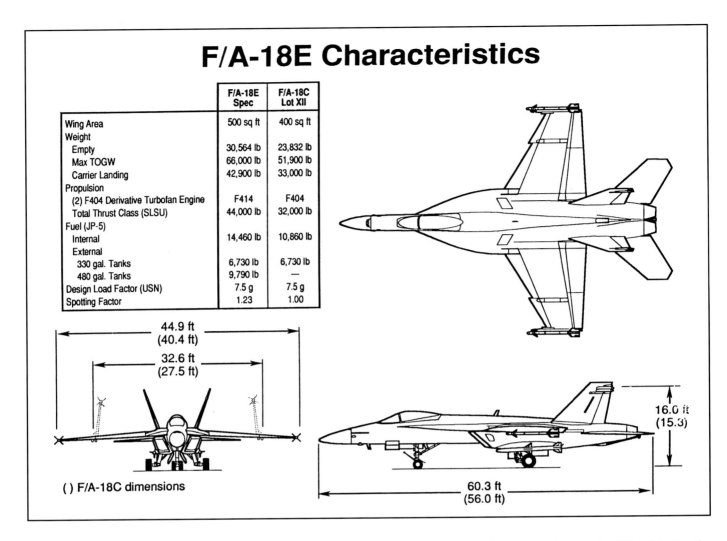

F/A-18E Characteristics

	F/A-18E Spec	F/A-18C Lot XII
Wing Area	500 sq ft	400 sq ft
Weight		
Empty	30,564 lb	23,832 lb
Max TOGW	66,000 lb	51,900 lb
Carrier Landing	42,900 lb	33,000 lb
Propulsion		
(2) F404 Derivative Turbofan Engine	F414	F404
Total Thrust Class (SLSU)	44,000 lb	32,000 lb
Fuel (JP-5)		
Internal	14,460 lb	10,860 lb
External		
330 gal. Tanks	6,730 lb	6,730 lb
480 gal. Tanks	9,790 lb	—
Design Load Factor (USN)	7.5 g	7.5 g
Spotting Factor	1.23	1.00

44.9 ft
(40.4 ft)

32.6 ft
(27.5 ft)

( ) F/A-18C dimensions

16.0 ft
(15.3)

60.3 ft
(56.0 ft)

The general F/A-18E characteristics as released by Boeing in 1995, with a parenthetical comparison to the F/A-18C. For the most part, the aircraft is the same today. (Boeing)

avionics related. In a most basic sense, the three primary redesign elements of the E/F are larger wings, a stretched fuselage, and higher-thrust engines. To accommodate more fuel, and thus increase the Super Hornet's range over that of the C/D, the fuselage was stretched by 2 feet 10 inches, thereby allowing carriage of 33 percent more internal fuel. To accommodate the higher carrier weight and provide the added lift, the Super Hornet's wing is a full 25 percent larger than that of the C/D (500 square feet in area and 4 feet 2.5 inches added span) and returns to the leading-edge "dogtooth" that was removed from the

A/B because of flutter problems. Since the Super Hornet's wing is thicker, flutter is less of a concern.

The larger wings also mean more room for weapons. A third wing station was added increasing the total number of stations from nine to eleven. Rated at 1,250 lbs., these new stations (Nos. 2 and 10) outboard the existing pylons, and can carry air-to-air and air-to-ground weapons, but are not plumbed for external fuel tanks. The larger wings also permit carriage of the larger 480-gallon external tanks aboard carriers, which then permits the Super Hornet (while using an ARS pod) to be

configured as a tanker. This wing design also solves the requirement for greater payload – a total of 17,000 lbs. can be carried externally, an increase of 20 percent.

Besides being larger, the E/F's wings are of a less complicated design, featuring one less spar and fewer ribs. The tail-section was also enlarged. Horizontal stabilators were increased in size by 36 percent and the vertical stabilizers (the tailfins) were increased by 15 percent. The speed brake, usually mounted between the tailfins, was removed and functionally replaced by deflecting the spoilers (located on each

LEX) up, the ailerons down, the trailing-edge flaps down, and toeing the rudders out. Rudder area was also increased by 54 percent and each can be deflected an additional 10 degrees to a total of 40 degrees.

Although not part of the original EMD design, the leading-edge extension (LEX) was also lengthened and recontoured in late 1992 in order to restore the degree of AoA maneuverability of the F/A-18C. LEX area increased from 62.4 square feet on the C/D to 75.3 square feet on the E/F. Located on the LEX are new spoilers and vents, which provide added control. The spoilers are located on the upper surface of each LEX and, in combination with other flight controls, act as a speed brake. The LEX spoilers are also used to enhance nose-down pitching moment at higher angles-of-attack.

Other structural changes included a strengthened and simplified undercarriage to accommodate the increased overall weight of the aircraft. To offset these, weight reductions were accomplished by using carbon epoxy panels in place of aluminum and by eliminating the mechanical flight-control back-up systems used by the C/D.

SURVIVABILITY

The aircraft's survivability has been enhanced significantly over the C/D through a variety of modifications. Due to its high cost, and the desire to avoid technologies that might be someday defeated, stealth was not heavily invested in as the Super Hornet's savior. This has obviously sparked much criticism of the Super Hornet as an aircraft that cannot deliver "first-day-of-the-war" sorties. However, survivability is not limited to stealthy low-observables.

What the E/F seeks to accomplish is a significantly reduced signature that allows it to effectively deliver stand-off weapons.

CDR Rob Niewoehner, the Navy's former lead test pilot on the E/F, explains this in a recent article in *Wings of Gold* magazinetating that:

"Stealth is one approach to survivability – a very expensive approach, whose stand-alone effectiveness is limited to a few mission scenarios. A flexible airplane requires a flexible approach to survivability, one that will deliver significant survivability improvements across the full span of envisioned missions. By balancing the survivability of the E/F (with a combination of reduction in its vulnerable area; signature reduction; employment of defensive system; and integration of

stand-off munitions such as JDAM, JSOW, and SLAM-ER), the airplane capitalizes on all the survivability technologies of the past decade."

The Super Hornet has many features geared to improve its chances of survival in high threat environments. Structurally, efforts were made to reduce the aircraft's overall radar signature by using a combination of radar-absorbing materials (RAM) and redesigned panels and engine inlets. RAM is used widely throughout the aircraft. Engine inlets were configured to a "caret" shape (angled box) as opposed to the "D-shaped" inlets used on the C/D and supply the engines with 172 lb./sec. of air flow rather that the 146 lb./sec. of air flow. Access panels and landing gear doors have been redesigned with jagged or "dog-toothed" edges to help deflect radar waves. According to sources,

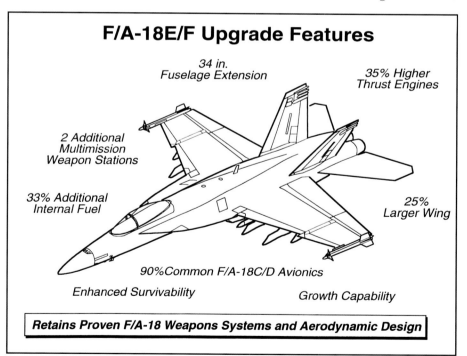

F/A-18E/F Upgrade Features

34 in. Fuselage Extension

35% Higher Thrust Engines

2 Additional Multimission Weapon Stations

33% Additional Internal Fuel

25% Larger Wing

90% Common F/A-18C/D Avionics

Enhanced Survivability

Growth Capability

Retains Proven F/A-18 Weapons Systems and Aerodynamic Design

Although retaining the basic shape of its predecessor, the E/F is a larger aircraft. This chart shows the major areas of distinction between the Hornet and Super Hornet. (Boeing)

radar signature has been reduced by an order of magnitude over the radar cross section of the most current F/A-18C/D models.

Internally, fire suppression gear has been added to reduce the incidence of fire and explosion, and environmentally friendly agent has been instituted for the Halon used by earlier aircraft. Vulnerability has also been decreased 14 percent by relocating and redesigning critical components.

The Super Hornet also features a sophisticated electronic defense system. Flare/chaff dispensers were doubled from two to four, with provisions for two additional dispensers. The quadruplex redundant fly-by-wire flight control system also makes the Super Hornet much more difficult to bring down by smaller caliber AAA and proximity fused warheads.

Survivability will be even further enhanced with the addition of the Integrated Defense Electronic Counter Measures (IDECM) System planned for 2004. The IDECM suite is comprised of the enhanced ALR-67(V)3 RWR, the ALQ-214 RF Countermeasures (RFCM) jammer, and the improved ALE-55 fiber-optic towed decoy jammer (FOTA). As the RFCM and ALE-55 are still under development, the Super Hornet will initially deploy with the ALE-50 towed decoy. Altogether these measures significantly improve the E/F's survivability.

Furthermore, the Super Hornet's added weapons stations and ability to carry more fuel means fewer sorties are required in to the target area and more tactically desirable routes are available. Niewoehner continued, "Fewer sorties and better routing will result in less threat exposure and enhanced survivability."

SUPER HORNET WEAPONS

Although configuration and carriage evaluations are still underway, the F/A-18E/F has been cleared for 59 by its first deployment. Twenty-nine configurations were presented for the Super Hornet OPEVAL, with others, such as the AIM-9X, to undergo Follow-on OPEVAL. Some of the weapons currently cleared include the AIM-7, AIM-9, and AIM-120 air-to-air missiles, the AGM-88 HARM, and AGM-84D Harpoon air-to-surface missiles, and a variety of iron and precision-guided bombs. As Captain Robert H. Rutherford, who was commander of VX-9 during the OPEVAL, has commented, "The weapons presented with the E/F at OPEVAL were the basic weapons we would use in a conflict." Once in the fleet it is expected that all 59 of the projected weapons configurations, which will include JDAM, JSOW, JASSM, AIM-9X, and

An unpainted F-2 makes its first flight on 11 October 1996. This aircraft is the sixth of the seven EMD aircraft to take to the air and was used for weapons testing. (Boeing)

other weapons currently on the drawing boards, will be cleared.

COCKPIT & AVIONICS

The initial Super Hornet configuration avionics remain 90 percent common with late model F/A-18C/Ds. Chief differences are in the cockpit layout, namely the display sizes and clarity and the touch-sensitive screens. Approximately 90 percent of the software components are compatible, as are 85 percent of the controls and displays, and 67 percent of the flight control system (due to the structural redesign).

To improve situational awareness, the 5-by-5 inch central display screen used by the C/D was replaced by a new Kaiser 8-by-8 inch flat panel active-matrix LCD display; the two monochrome MRDs (also 5-by-5 inch) used by the C/D were replaced by two multipurpose screens, also made by Kaiser. Finally, the up-front control (UFC) panel, used for communications and navigational controls, was replaced by a monochrome touch-sensitive screen. The E/F further features a new engine/fuel display with a programmable monochrome active-matrix LCD display that graphically displays nozzle positions and fuel tank capacity/fuel tank "bingo" in pounds.

Many have claimed that the E/F's avionics high degree of commonality with that of the C/D means that the Super Hornet is using "recycled 1970s technology." Again, Niewoehner explains this: "The F/A-18A/B/C/D's phenomenal growth in systems and missions are at the brink of physically exhausting the space of a 1970s airframe, while the weapons system inside is unquestionably 1990s. Modest

improvements from Lot XIX C/D to E/F are all that are initially required to make the Super Hornet state-of-the-art. What is needed is a 1990s airframe that can handle the growth for the avionics and weapons systems advances of the next five to 20 years. The F/A-18E/F is that airframe." This growth potential will allow adaptation of state-of-the-art weapons technologies that cannot be realized by modifying the C/D.

ENGINES

Two General Electric F414 afterburning turbofan engines provide power for the Super Hornet and are each capable of delivering up to 21,890 lbs. thrust. Derived from the F404 used in the original Hornet, the F414 incorporates technologies from the F412 engine developed for the canceled A-12 and also from GE's

advanced YF120 design. As compared to the F404, the F414 provides 16 percent higher airflow and has an increased overall 30:1 pressure ratio, and a 9:1 thrust-to-weight ratio, yet has the same length and aft diameter. Much of the increased performance comes through the use of an integrally bladed disk (called blisks) in the compressors.

Several features of the F414 are from other designs. The core, for example, was that developed for the F412. The afterburner derived from the YF120 and features air-cooled radial flameholders and an exhaust nozzle incorporating ceramic-matrix composite flaps and seals for increased engine life. Carbonfibre composites are used to control weight. Also new to the F/A-18E/F is the dual-channel full-authority digital electronic control (FADEC) system engine control.

Rated at 14,770-lbs. dry thrust and 21,890-lbs. with afterburner, the F414-GE-400 turbofan provides approximately 35 percent more thrust than the current F402 EPE engines through most of the flight envelope. The F414 was derived from the F412 core as developed for the A-12 and the low-pressure system from the YF120 developed for the YF-22 and YF-23. (Boeing)

Seen at the St. Louis plant is the nose section of F1, which will house the radar and gun. (Brad Elward)

One of the reasons that the Super Hornet has some 33 percent fewer parts than the C/D is due to advances in subassembly construction. Parts that were traditionally comprised of numerous subassemblies were built as a single unit through creative machining. These ribs are now one piece, whereas on C/Ds, they are made of dozens of parts fastened together. The one-piece assemblies are stronger, easier to build, and less expensive. (Brad Elward)

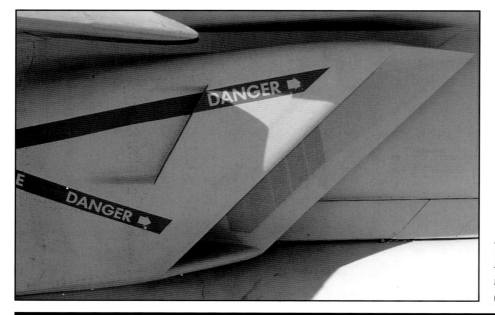

The engine intakes on the Super Hornet are wedge-shaped to reduce the aircraft's radar cross section. (Ted Carlson)

Boeing's 1995 Powerpoint™ presentation highlights the subsystem/avionics differences between the Hornet and Super Hornet. (Boeing)

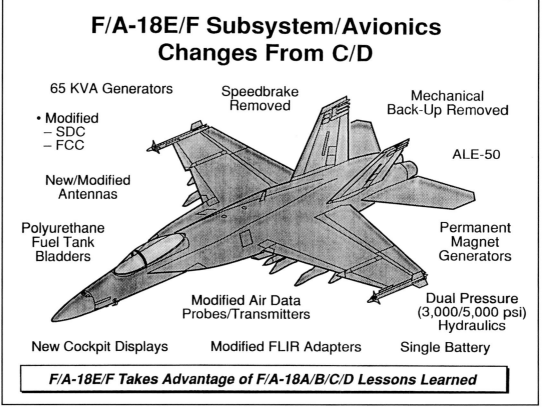

F/A-18E/F Subsystem/Avionics Changes From C/D

65 KVA Generators

Speedbrake Removed

Mechanical Back-Up Removed

- Modified
  – SDC
  – FCC

ALE-50

New/Modified Antennas

Polyurethane Fuel Tank Bladders

Permanent Magnet Generators

Modified Air Data Probes/Transmitters

Dual Pressure (3,000/5,000 psi) Hydraulics

New Cockpit Displays

Modified FLIR Adapters

Single Battery

F/A-18E/F Takes Advantage of F/A-18A/B/C/D Lessons Learned

The engines of this F/A-18E and tailhook assembly are clearly visible. A "remove-before-flight" tag hangs from the tailhook release at center photo. (Brad Elward)

During EMD carrier tests landing signal officers (LSOs) had trouble distinguishing between an approaching Super Hornet and an F/A-18C. The same problem had occurred with the Grumman EA-6B Prowler and the A-6 Intruder, which was solved by painting a small radiation symbol on the Prowler's radome. This was resolved on the Super Hornet by adding a new grouping of lights, seen here as three colored circles on the small rectangle. (Brad Elward)

The diamond-shaped areas around this angle-of-attack vane helps reduce radar cross section and represents one of the many small ways the Super Hornet's design compensates for the lack of stealth. (Ted Carlson)

The main landing gear well covers were redesigned with jagged edges (referred to as a faceted design) to help deflect radar emissions. (Ted Carlson)

F/A-18E/F Provides Additional Weapons Carriage Capability

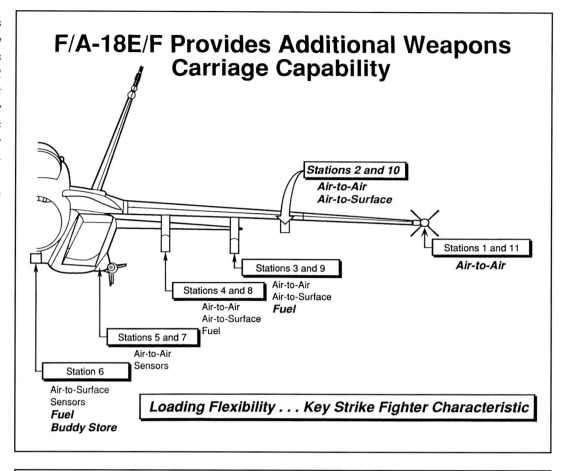

Stations 2 and 10
Air-to-Air
Air-to-Surface

Stations 1 and 11
Air-to-Air

Stations 3 and 9
Air-to-Air
Air-to-Surface
Fuel

Stations 4 and 8
Air-to-Air
Air-to-Surface
Fuel

Stations 5 and 7
Air-to-Air
Sensors

Station 6
Air-to-Surface
Sensors
Fuel
Buddy Store

Loading Flexibility . . . Key Strike Fighter Characteristic

F/A-18E/F Materials Usage

Percent of Structural Weight

	F/A-18C/D	F/A-18E/F
☐ Aluminum	49	31
▧ Steel	15	14
▥ Titanium	13	21
▦ Carbon Epoxy	10	19
☐ Other	13	15
	100	100

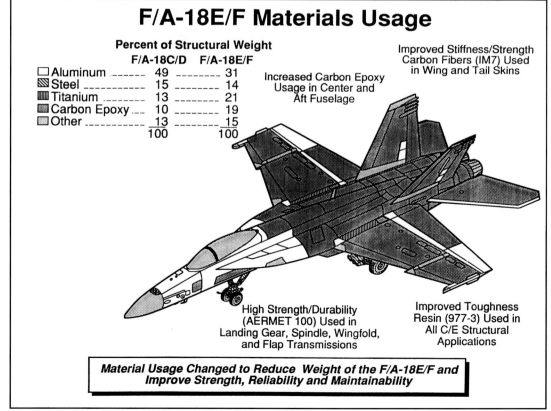

Improved Stiffness/Strength Carbon Fibers (IM7) Used in Wing and Tail Skins

Increased Carbon Epoxy Usage in Center and Aft Fuselage

High Strength/Durability (AERMET 100) Used in Landing Gear, Spindle, Wingfold, and Flap Transmissions

Improved Toughness Resin (977-3) Used in All C/E Structural Applications

Material Usage Changed to Reduce Weight of the F/A-18E/F and Improve Strength, Reliability and Maintainability

The Martin-Baker Navy Aircrew Common Ejection Seat (NACES) SJU-17-1/A is capable of zero-zero ejection, which means that a pilot can escape even while sitting on the ramp or during a cold cat launch. (Brad Elward)

This head-on view of the Super Hornet cockpit reveals the larger screens and the new fuel display at lower left. The Up-Front Control panel is at top center and controls navigation and communications. (Brad Elward)

FLIGHT 6 TESTS

AND THE OPERATIONAL EVALUATION

With its first flight in November 1995 under its belt, the Super Hornet was now well on its way to entering fleet service. As the production of the seven contracted Super Hornets continued, focus shifted to proving that the aircraft could live up to its advertised capabilities. Indeed, the primary objectives of the EMD phase as a whole are to "translate the most promising design into a stable, producible, cost-effective design; validate the manufacturing processes; and demonstrate system capabilities through testing." In laymen terms, this means to "detect what was not predicted and to fix what goes wrong."

After additional preliminary flight tests in St. Louis, the next step for the Super Hornet during the EMD was the development flight test program. Conducted at the Naval Air Warfare Center at NAS Patuxent River, Maryland, the program used seven Hornets: five single-seat E models and two two-seat F models. Three ground test articles were also part of the study as was an F/A-18D fitted with new avionics to serve as an avionics testbed. As a testament to its careful design, the Super Hornet entered EMD flight testing 1,000 lbs. under projected weight.

THE SUPER HORNET GOES TO PAX RIVER

The development flight test phase of the EMD began in February 1996 conducted by an Integrated Test Team (ITT). The Super Hornet's EMD phase was unique in that it combined Navy and contractor flight testing under one program, rather than having two independent tests proceed consecutively. Engineers and test pilots from both groups worked side-by-side, directly exchanging their impressions and findings. Support was also given by elements of the Navy's Operational Test and Evaluation Squadron, VX-9. By doing this, the EMD test flight phase was reduced by as much as one year. This program has now become the model for all future EMD programs, including the new JSF.

CDR Dave Dunaway, who served as the VX-9 ITT liaison during the latter part of the developmental flight tests, says the ITT's work at this

Seven EMD aircraft participated in flight tests at NAS Patuxent River. E4 (BuNo. 165168) was charged with high angles-of-attack evaluations. It has been painted white and orange to provide high visibility for ground tracking cameras. The spin chute is visible between the vertical tails. (Boeing)

As part of the initial carrier qualifications, F1 headed to USS John C. Stennis (CVN-74) in January 1997 for a week of sea trials. The aircraft performed magnificently and no software changes were needed. (Boeing)

stage "sought to show that the aircraft can fly, that it can fight, and that its systems can work together."

The first test flight occurred on 4 March 1996. As proof of the pace at which the EMD phase moved forward, the EMD Super Hornets had accumulated 3,000 flight hours and had expanded the flight envelope beyond 50,000 feet, speeds greater than Mach 1.5, and +7/-1.7 Gs.

CQs Prove Reliability Around the Boat

Preparation for the Super Hornet's first sea trials began in mid-1996 at NAS Patuxent River, Maryland, where, on 6 August CDR Tom Gurney piloted the F/A-18 F1 in the Super Hornet's first catapult launch from a land-based, steam powered MK-7 catapult. On 21 August, F1 made the first arrested landing in a Super Hornet, also at Patuxent River.

Following extensive carrier suitability testing at the Navy's Lakehurst New Jersey facilities during February and March 1998, F/A-18F1 headed out to USS *John S. Stennis* (CVN-74) in January 1997 for the Super Hornet's initial sea trials. Despite cold and snowy weather off the coast of Cape Hateras, North Carolina, F1 made the two-hour flight from the Naval Air Warfare Center at Patuxent River and landed in what were considered "challenger" weather conditions for an aircraft at this stage of its flight tests. The first carrier landing was made by Navy LT Frank Morley on 18 January at approxi-

---

SUPER HORNET EMD DEVELOPMENT AIRCRAFT

As with most flight test programs, each Super Hornet was given specific primary duties:

Aircraft	First Flight	EMD Flight Assignments
E1 165164	29 November 1995	investigate flying qualities and expand flight envelope
E2 165165	26 December 1995	engine and performance testing
F1 165166	1 April 1996	carrier suitability & later weapons testing
E3 165167	2 January 1997	load testing
E4 165168	2 July 1996	high AOA evaluations
F2 165169	11 October 1996	weapons testing (had full avionics suite)
E5 165170	27 August 1996	first with full mission capability; weapons separation testing

mately 10:00 a.m. EST; CDR Tom Gurney, who manned the F/A-18B chase plane for the initial trap, then switched places with Morley and made the Super Hornet's first carrier catapult launch at approximately 2:30 p.m. that same day.

The two pilots made 61 daytime launches and recoveries during the six-day deployment, examining flying qualities from behind the ship, dual and single-engine handling, and trim and crosswind effects when coming off the bow and waist catapults. A total of 54 touch-and-go landings were also made. Car-Quals demonstrated a landing approach speed of 10 knots slower than the C/D, which further enhances the E/F's safety margin and handling characteristics around the boat. The pilots described their experiences, stating that the Super Hornet had "[g]reat hands-off flyaway characteristics off the catapult" and that it "[flew] well on approach, as expected, despite challenging wind conditions."

Weapons Separation Tests

Two Super Hornets – E5 and F2 – were assigned to weapons separation testing during the EMD. Although the phase began in October, 1996, the first separations test did not take place until 19 February 1997 when F1 successfully released an empty 480-gallon fuel tank from 5,000 feet. Two days later, Northrop Grumman test pilot Jim Sandberg flew E1 with stores, marking the first time a Super Hornet carried a simulated warload. E1 flew with an "Aero Servo Elasticity" stores configuration comprised of three 480-gallon tanks, two AIM-9s, two Mk-84 iron bombs, and two HARMs. Weighing some 62,400 lbs., this load represented the largest gross weight

to date of the program. Sandberg commented that the plane flew great: "The airplane flew effortlessly throughout the flight" and "performed as if it were flying clean."

In early April, F1 launched the first air-to-air missile – an AIM-9 Sidewinder – followed by the launch of an AIM-120 on 5 May. By late May, the Super Hornet had successfully released AIM-7, flares from the ALE-47 dispenser, SLAM, Harpoon, a ripple of 10 MK-82s; MK-83s, a dual load of CBU-100s, and ejected 480-gallon tanks from both wing and the centerline stations. The ALE-50 towed decoy had also been tested. Flights continued into 1998 and 1999, with live firings of HARMs in December 1998 and Harpoon launch

in January 1999 against a moving ship. By the end of the EMD weapons separation phase, 25 missiles had been fired and over 500,000 lbs. of ordnance. Eventually, 29 weapons configurations were cleared and made available during OPEVAL. A total of 59 should be cleared by VFA-115's first cruise in 2001.

Fleet Introduction Team (FIT)

As the Super Hornet progressed through its initial flight tests with the ITT, the Navy activated a Fleet Introduction Team (FIT) at NAS Lemoore under the initial leadership of CDR Phil Tomkins. The FIT's first order of business was to refurbish hangars and ready rooms necessary for the reactivation of VFA-122 in 1998.

The F/A-18E entered EMD flight testing approximately 1,000 lbs. underweight and remains approximately 480 lbs. underweight today. The EMD is essentially the period when evaluators confirm aircraft performance and attempt to discover and fix problems that were not predicted. (Boeing)

The Super Hornet can carry three external fuel tanks and still have four wing, two fuselage, and two wingtip stations available for weapons. The slight outward cant of the inboard tanks, represented a minor modification to reduce separation problems. (Boeing via Dennis R. Jenkins)

Formerly an A-7 Fleet Readiness Squadron until disestablished in 1991, VFA-122 was recommissioned in January 1999 and now stands as the sole Super Hornet FRS. VFA-122 is responsible for creating the Super Hornet training syllabus and for developing the tactics needed to employ the Super Hornet in line with its capabilities. The squadron began training future instructors in 1999 and received its first "students" in June 2000. New classes began every 6 weeks thereafter. CAPT Scott Swift is currently the Commanding Officer of VFA-122. Although plans once called for the establishment of an East Coast E/F FRS (likely VFA-174), recent Navy comments now suggest that Lemoore will be the sole site.

FINAL CQS ABOARD THE *TRUMAN*

The Super Hornet returned to sea for the final pre-OPEVAL CarQuals in February and March 1999 aboard USS *Harry S. Truman*, (CVN-75) again in the Atlantic, but off the coast of Florida. During these operations, Navy pilot LCDR Lance Floyd made the F/A-18F's first night time carrier landing. Both Fs were flown during this at-sea period. The Super Hornet was successfully launched off the bow with 15 knots of crosswind and off the waist catapult with 10 knots crosswind. Launches and traps were also made with various asymmetrical weapons configurations and using the automatic carrier landing approach system from distances of 4 and 8 miles out.

Other flights included "minimum end speed" tests with military power and full afterburner. These are some of the highest risk tests with a goal of determining the lowest take-off speeds possible. It can be

unnerving for those pilots to be launched and feel the aircraft sink, as it is only 65 feet to the water. At its max gross weight, (66,000 lbs.) the F was able to launch with full afterburner at 142 knots, and reportedly sank only ten feet below the bow before recovering. The aircraft was noted to handle "superbly" and was very responsive to last-minute corrections.

EMD PROBLEMS

Most flight test programs find something deficient in the tested platform and tests of the Super Hornet proved no exception. In fact, by December 1997, less than a year and nine months into the EMD flight tests, the ITT had identified over 400 deficiencies (again, less than the A/B). The most significant deficiencies impacted the aircraft's flying qualities, service life, engine performance, and weapons separation.

Although there were the usual delays in the flight test program for inclement weather and maintenance, the program experienced two delays that were significant and quite unexpected. The first delay took place during the summer of 1996 and involved the delivery of the final three EMD aircraft. This delay resulted from a three-month machinists strike at one of the major contractor's facilities. The second delay occurred in 1997, following a serious in-flight engine malfunction, which curtailed all flight tests (except those of F1 to determine carrier suitability) for two months.

Other problems developed during the course of the EMD flight tests that slowed its progress. Perhaps the most publicized was the "wing drop" phenomenon that first appeared in March 1996. This phe-

nomenon was formally described as "an unacceptable, uncommanded abrupt lateral roll that randomly occurs at the altitude and speed at which air-to-air combat maneuvers are expected to occur." Wing drop is caused by airflow separating on one wing before the other and typically occurred when the aircraft was maneuvered at relatively high angles-of-attack and high g-forces. A common phenomenon on high-performance, swept-wing aircraft, the problem was first noticed during the 1950s on the F-86. The reason this problem drew so much attention was because it is impossible to predict these phenomena in the laboratory. As a result, the only way to evaluate fixes is to fly them. Until the solution was found, there was no way to know for sure whether a complete wing design was needed or not.

ITT personnel explored the extent of the problem until mid-1997. Test flights placed the wing drop in the center of the Super Hornet's flight envelope – between Mach 0.70 and 0.95 at altitudes of 10,000 to 40,000 feet and angles-of-attack between 6 and 12 degrees. Efforts to resolve the problem ran from July through December, with ITT members joining forces with Navy and Boeing engineers, as well as experts from the Air Force, academe, and NASA.

Initially, the problem was so severe that further expansion of the flight envelope was impossible. An interim solution found on modifications to the leading-edge flaps and flight control software reduced the severity of the problem by 80 percent, thus allowing continuation of the flight tests. However, the real solution came by adding porous wing-fold fairings, which wrung out the remaining 20 percent, making the aircraft acceptable for fleet introduction. According to Boeing documents, "The porous fairing has many small holes that influence the airflow over the wing, eliminating wing drop throughout the maneuvering envelope." Engineers experimented with several designs before settling on the final version found on production models.

Weapons separation problems were also noticed during the EMD phase. Early wind tunnel tests conducted during July and August 1993 showed that some stores would collide with the side of the fuselage or other stores when released. This was caused by adverse air flow created by the E/F airframe. To cure the problem, the pylons were redesigned and toed slightly outward. Subsequent tests proved the redesign corrected most of the problem. Another related deficiency was with unwanted noise and vibration. For fear of structural damage, speed limitations have been placed on the Super Hornet when carrying certain weapons. While some of these remain today and were noted during the subse-

F1 made 64 arrested landings and catapult launches and 54 "touch-and-goes" during its five-day sea trial period aboard USS John C. Stennis. (Boeing)

This Super Hornet carries two Sidewinders, two HARMs, two JSOWs, and two Mk 83 bombs. (Boeing via Dennis R. Jenkins)

quent OPEVAL, the Navy and Boeing have decided it is more economical to redesign the weapons to handle the additional noise.

THE OPEVAL

Beginning 27 May 1999, the Super Hornet entered the long-awaited Operational Test and Evaluation (OPEVAL) that concluded in November that same year. The goal of any program heading through an OPEVAL is to receive the highest rating of "operationally effective" and "operationally suitable". *Operationally effective* means that aircraft is able to perform its mission in the fleet environment and in the face of unexpected threats, including countermeasures. *Operationally suitable*

means that the aircraft, when operated and maintained by typical fleet personnel in the expected numbers and of the expected experience level, is supportable when deployed. For the F/A-18E/F, this meant that the aircraft would be ready for the fleet and further cleared the way for full-rate production.

The OPEVAL used the 1991 Navy Operation Requirement Document (ORD) for the F/A-18E/F Upgrade as a guide. OR demanded the following improvements over the existing F/A-18C/D: (1) increased mission radius; (2) increased payload flexibility; (3) increased carrier recovery or "bringback;" (4) increased survivability; and (5) decreased vulnerability. Improvements in combat perfor-

mance over the Lot XII F/A-18 C/D and growth capability were a must.

THE GROUND RULES

The OPEVAL was performed on the F/A-18E/F "as is", without reference to the systems not yet in place, such as AESA, AIM-9X, or the JHMCS. Moreover, no consideration was given to new systems on the books designed to replace legacy systems such as the ATFLIR, SHARP, or ATARS. CDR Dave Dunaway described this as taking "basically an immature aircraft, one in its infancy, and pitting it against established threat systems." Thus, what was tested does not fully respond to full Super Hornet capability. Seven Super Hornets participated in the

OPEVAL. These included the first three F/A-18Es and four F/A-18Fs delivered under the LRIP Lot 1 contract. The OPEVAL tests were flown by a team of 14 pilots and 9 WSOs, who came from several backgrounds, including the F/A-18, F-14, S-3, A-6, and A-7 communities. An additional 70 Navy personnel were assigned to perform maintenance.

FIVE-PHASE TEST PROGRAM

VX-9 conducted a five-phase test program designed to test the Super Hornet under realistic operating conditions to determine the effectiveness and suitability of the aircraft, its systems, and its weapons for combat. All primary missions of the E/F – interdiction, war-at-sea, fighter escort, CAP, alert interceptor, air combat maneuvering (ACM), SEAD, CAS, tanker, and FAC(A) – were evaluated with the exception of reconnaissance. Following an initial period when the OPEVAL aircrews familiarized themselves with the aircraft at China Lake, the evaluators were ready to go. The five phases were as follows:

1. Air-to-ground Phase

This Phase began on 27 May at China Lake and involved flights to evaluate the Super Hornet with air-to-ground weapons and sensors, defense suppression, and survivability.

While not all of the weapons planned for the E/F were cleared for OPEVAL, those 29 distinct payload configurations that were cleared were representative of the configurations to be fielded. Super Hornets delivered Mk 82 (500 lbs.) and Mk 83 (1,000 lbs.) iron bombs as well as cluster bombs (CBUs), and also demonstrated their proficiency at tanking on both day and night mis-

sions. Various range profiles were also flown to verify the flight performance data.

2. Air Combat Phase

This Phase was conducted as a two-week detachment at NAS Key West, Florida, from 14-25 June. Adversary support was provided by F-16Cs of the 185th Fighter Squadron, ANG from Sioux City, Iowa, which flew a series a realistic threat tactics emulating the latest generation MiG-29. VX-9 evaluated the Super Hornet in a variety of fighter escort and CAP profiles and ACM regimes and further assessed tactics and survivability. Some scenarios pitted up to four Super Hornets against an equal or larger number of threat adversaries. Mixed sections of Hornet and Super Hornets were also flown to compare the performance of the two aircraft under similar conditions.

3. Carrier Operations

A detachment from VX-9 took Super Hornets to USS *Abraham Lincoln* from 12–28 July to evaluate the aircraft's flight characteristics around the boat and to see how it integrated with a carrier air wing. The first several days were spent qualifying the aircrews. During the remaining period, the Super Hornets flew as a mini-squadron with other CVW-9 aircraft where the Super Hornet's performance and ability to integrate could be monitored. Simulated alert launches, tanking, and strikes were all flown by VX-9 crews. The Super Hornet integrated well and fulfilled all tasked missions.

4. Combined/Joint Operations

The final detachment took place at Nellis AFB, Nevada, from 16-27 August as the Super Hornets partici-

The long-range air-to-air weapon of the Super Hornet is the AIM-120 AMRAAM. Here, F2 completes the first live-fire test on 5 May 1997. (Vernon Pugh, USN via Boeing)

One solution explored included use of an 18-in. "grit" strip on the leading-edge inboard of the dog-tooth. (Boeing)

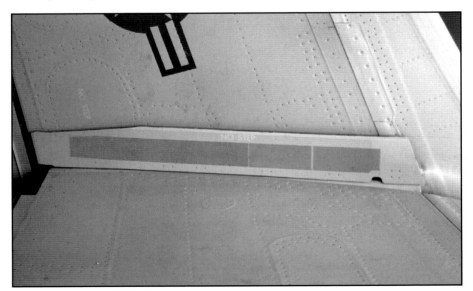

The "wing drop" phenomenon was one of the most highly publicized EMD problems. Many solutions were conceived and tested, but the answer came by adding a porous fairing over the wingfold mechanism. This fairing solved the wing drop problem, but some buffeting resulted that is still being investigated. (Boeing)

pated in a Combined/Joint Red Flag Exercise. Units from the Air Force, Marines, Navy, and several foreign countries participated in creating a highly realistic scenario representative of the NATO missions flown today. All flights were conducted with instrument pods for later review, although some live ordnance was used. Flights also assessed the Super Hornet's performance in the strike, SEAD, fighter escort, and interdiction roles.

5. Survivability, Air-to-air Missile & Smart Weapons

The final stage focused on survivability flights and was conducted at China Lake from September through November 1999. Operationally representative flights were flown against actual and surrogate threat SAMs, followed by air-to-ground gunnery and air-to-ground flights.

The OPEVAL officially ended in November with CDR Jeff Penfield, future Executive Officer of VFA-115, making the final flight. Over 850 sorties were flown with a total of 1,233 flight hours, and approximately 400,000 lbs. of ordnance was expended. The reduced vulnerability was demonstrated against a variety of threat munitions.

This represents the porous fairing on production models. (Brad Elward)

VX-9 Releases its Findings

Following review of the OPEVAL ratings and report, the results were announced on 15 February 2000 by Rear Admiral John B. Nathman, Director of Air Warfare in the Office of the Chief of Naval Operations. The VX-9 report found the Super Hornet "operationally effective and operationally suitable" and recommended the aircraft's introduction into fleet service. Several areas of "significant enhancement" were noted, ranging from tactical flexibility (including that of tanker), payload flexibility, carrier performance, and survivability. Maneuvering and handling qualities were high and the aircraft was noted to resist departure even under aggressive high-AoA maneuvering. Another enhanced quality is known as positive nose pointing, which means how fast a pilot can put his aircraft nose on a target. This quality is outstanding in the Super Hornet and it allows the pilot to quickly put the aircraft's nose on a bogie at virtually all AoAs and airspeeds. Weapons delivering accuracy was also reported "excellent and in excess of the ORD accuracy requirements."

In regards to performance, the E/F is comparable or superior to the C/D in turns, climbs, and deceleration at subsonic speeds. However, in the transonic/supersonic regime, the E/F experiences large accelerations (airspeed bleed-off) during maneuvering. This is said to be tactically insignificant since most maneuvering in an engagement rapidly migrates to the "current of the flight envelope" (approximately 0.86 Mach at 15,000 feet). Moreover, the Super Hornet is almost immune to departure, making it extremely valuable during a close-in fight. To the surprise of some, evaluators detected none of the "wing drop" phenomenon experienced during EMD. The residual lateral activity reported by the press was of minimal concern to the VX-9 evaluators.

One area of concern voiced by NAVAIR notes the limited number of specific stores configurations cleared. In his statement to the Senate Armed Services Committee, AirLand Forces Subcommittee on 22 March 2000, Phillip E. Coyle, Director, Operational Test & Evaluation noted:

"Air-to-air missiles could not be employed if they were carried on a store station adjacent to air-to-ground ordnance. Numerous munitions could be carried and/or employed only from selected stores stations, although the plan is to bear these munitions from other stations as well."

"Consequently," Coyle concluded, "many of the load advantages planned for the F/A-18 E/F were not demonstrated during OPEVAL." Nevertheless, many of the configurations presented to OPEVAL were beyond the capabilities of current F/A-18C. Additional stores configurations will be cleared in support of the E/F's first deployment in scheduled follow-on tests and evaluations.

The black and white triangles and circles are for monitoring weapons separation. Note the cameras (red) mounted on the wingtip stations. (Boeing)

F1 sits perched on the starboard bow cat during initial sea trials. The F/A-18B was never trialed aboard carriers. Later, when the Marines adapted the two-place "D" for tactical operations, there was simply no money in the budget to qualify the D for Navy use. This was factored into the use of a two-place Super Hornet for sea trials. (Boeing)

Taken during OpEval, this Super Hornet participates in air wing strikes to see how the F/A-18F integrates into normal carrier operations. (Boeing)

READY FOR ACTION

THE SUPER HORNET ENTERS SERVICE

Stood up in January 1999, VFA-122 officially opened its doors to the first Super Hornet class in June 2000 and, at the time of this writing, is busy training air crews for VFA-115, which will make the first Super Hornet cruise aboard USS *Abraham Lincoln* (CVN-72) in 2001. The second Hornet cruise is slated for USS *Nimitz* in 2003 and will involve at least one Super Hornet squadron, most likely an F. Precisely which squadrons will transition to the F/A-18E/F and in what order is still being determined, but priority is being given first to squadrons operating the older F-14As, F/A-18As, and finally the F-14Bs and -Ds. VF-41 will be the first F-14 squadron to transition. As proof of how quickly Navy plans change, just a few years ago the first operational fleet Super Hornet squadron was to transition from the F-14A into the F/A-18F.

FUTURE GROWTH

As noted in the previous discussion of the OPEVAL's recommendations, the Super Hornet is still an aircraft which has yet to realize its great potential for growth. Thus, numerous systems are needed to realize the E/F's full combat capability. These systems include development and acquisition of SHARP, the AIM-9X/JHMCS system, MIDS, AESA, APX-111 CIT, and ATFLIR.

According to Boeing's Paul Summers, F/A-18 New Products Development Manager, the baseline for E/F avionics as it enters service is the C/D Block 19 standard. This includes the APG-73 radar, as well as the ability to incorporate MIDS, ATFLIR, and the JHMCS. The E/F avionics and electronics essentially provide a new infrastructure for continued development of the Super Hornet platform.

Summers indicated that a two Block upgrade is currently planned for the E/F beginning in 2005, which will incorporate several new avionics features and serve as the baseline for all future Super Hornet derivatives, including the proposed F/A-18G. At this point, the Block I upgrade is to include new mission computers to replace the current AYK-14 computers, which have basically run out of memory. These new computers will incorporate commercial-based processors and will bring greater processing power, more memory, and will feature open-architecture,

McDonnell Douglas (now Boeing) began exploring use of the F/A-18F as an electronic warfare platform in 1993 with limited Navy funding. When that funding ceased, Boeing assumed the study itself, and later joined forces with Northrop Grumman, the manufacturer of the EA-6B Prowler. This computer-illustration depicts an electronic warfare variant of the Super Hornet, which has been referred to as the Growler. Boeing contemplated using a single multi-band jamming pod to replace all five ALQ-99 pods used by the Prowler, leaving the remaining stations open for hard-kill ordnance. This undertaking proved exceedingly expensive and more recent efforts by Boeing have focused on reusing ICAP-III technologies and adapting the ALQ-99 pods for supersonic flight. (Boeing)

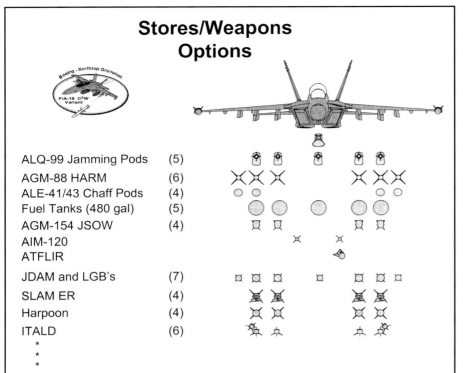

Stores/Weapons Options

ALQ-99 Jamming Pods	(5)
AGM-88 HARM	(6)
ALE-41/43 Chaff Pods	(4)
Fuel Tanks (480 gal)	(5)
AGM-154 JSOW	(4)
AIM-120	
ATFLIR	
JDAM and LGB's	(7)
SLAM ER	(4)
Harpoon	(4)
ITALD	(6)
*	
*	
*	

The Growler proposal will retain a lethal hard-kill capability, allowing it to take out radar and SAM installations on its own, and also allowing self-escort through carriage of air-to-air missiles. The Growler can carry three pods and still carry up to four HARMs or a combination of HARMs and JSOW or SLAM. (Boeing)

thereby allowing easy upgrade as new technology evolves. The two MFDs carried over from the C/D will be replaced by an advanced display. The added processing power of the new computers will allow engineers to eliminate the so-called "smart" displays, and replace them with "dumb" displays that receive their data from the mission computers via a broadband high-speed data bus. Another important change brought by the planned Block II upgrade is a new larger 200 by 250 mm color LCD for the rear cockpit. The aft cockpit hand controllers will also be modified to allow the WSO to release weapons.

Integration of the IDECM and decoupled cockpits are also essential, as is placing priority on clearing all of the planned stores configurations. The decoupled cockpits, also called independent crew stations, will allow F/A-18F crews to perform air-to-air and air-to-ground missions

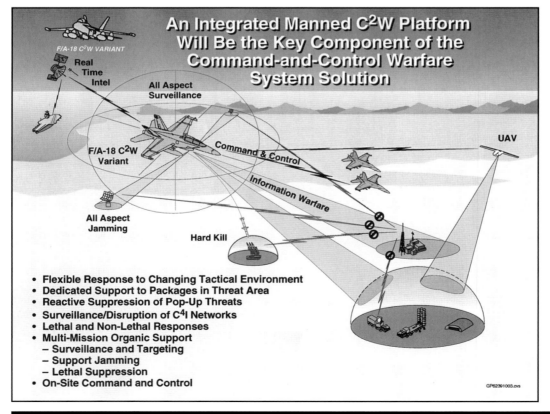

An Integrated Manned C^{2}W Platform Will Be the Key Component of the Command-and-Control Warfare System Solution

- Flexible Response to Changing Tactical Environment
- Dedicated Support to Packages in Threat Area
- Reactive Suppression of Pop-Up Threats
- Surveillance/Disruption of C^{4}I Networks
- Lethal and Non-Lethal Responses
- Multi-Mission Organic Support
  - Surveillance and Targeting
  - Support Jamming
  - Lethal Suppression
- On-Site Command and Control

A Boeing illustration highlights the advantages of the integrated manned C2W platform. (Boeing)

ALQ-99 tactical jamming pods are loaded on to Super Hornet F1 at NAS Patuxent River to evaluate fit. Above photo depicts five pods, plus two HARMs and two AMRAAMs. The photo at right represents three pods, with two HARMs, two AMRAAMS, and two JSOW. (Boeing)

simultaneously. Scheduled for introduction in 2004, crews using the decoupled system will be able to independently guide and control various weapons and on-board sensors. Also part of the upgrade, MIDS allows integration of secure, jam-resistant Link 16, thereby providing Super Hornet crews with off-board sensor data from land-based and air-based platforms, such as E-2C Hawkeyes. Modifications to the APG-73 will also be completed (until AESA follows) incorporating RUG II SAR modes for generating highly accurate ground maps. These modes are now only available on the F/A-18D used by the Marine Corps.

THE ELECTRONIC "GROWLER"

Although an Analysis of Alternatives program is still under way and not expected to yield a decision under December 2001, much talk has been made of configuring the two-seat "F" for the electronic warfare role to replace the Grumman EA-6B Prowler. Without question, the importance of electronic warfare has grown with the proliferation of advanced air defense networks. During the Gulf War and over Kosovo and Yugoslavia, Prowlers proved indispensable and most missions

were on a "go/no go" status depending on Prowler availability.

Boeing refers to the electronic version of the F/A-18F as the Command & Control Warfare (C2W) or Airborne Electronic Attack (AEA) variant (also called by some the F/A-18G), and work has been ongoing since 1993 when budgetary cuts associated with defense down-sizing forced the Navy to cancel the planned AVCAP upgrade program for the EA-6B fleet. As a result, the Navy began looking for alternatives and funded a study to determine whether the new F/A-18F could be made into a suitable electronic warfare platform. Although the study was funded for only a short while, McDonnell Douglas continued on the program, later adding Northrop Grumman as the electronic warfare systems integrator.

McDonnell Douglas submitted its original proposal to the Naval Air Systems Command in November 1997. Calling for the use of a new single multi-band jamming pod to replace the five ALQ-99 Tactical Jamming System (TJS) pods used by the EA-6B, the development costs were steep at over $2 billion. The Navy balked at this figure and asked McDonnell Douglas to refocus its efforts on a more affordable alternative using a combination of commercial-off-the-shelf (COTS) technologies and other hardware planned for the ICAP III EA-6B upgrades. This new emphasis shed the most expensive features of the proposed C2W variant and reduced proposed program costs by nearly 60 percent.

Key elements of the C2W proposal include SATCOM, the addition of low-band electronic surveillance antennas, wingtip-mounted receiver pods, and incorporation of the USQ-113 communications receiver from the ICAP III program. Most avionics changes would be software-related to accommodate the new electronic warfare mission. By using a high degree of automation and enhanced displays, the C2W will be able to perform all the missions of the four-person EA-6B crew with the two-person F/A-18G crew. Boeing has already established a reconfigured simulator in St. Louis and has been testing these automated concepts on fleet EA-6B Electronic Counter Measures Operators (ECMOs). Also planned for the C2W is use of the APG-79 AESA radar, which will provide a high-powered jammer/receiver in the frequency band of the radar. This radar can then be used for suppression jamming or passive attack, or in the conventional air-to-air/air-to-ground role.

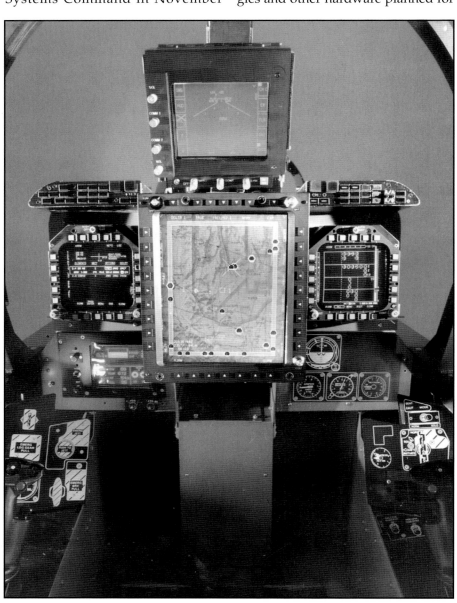

One feature of the C2W also planned for the F is the advanced crew station. A 10 x 10-inch color display will replace the 6.25 x 6.25 inch displays used by current D models and new Fs. This new display should be available in 2005. (Boeing)

Tests were conducted in 1999 using the current ALQ-99 TJS pods on one of the EMD F/A-18Fs at NAS Patuxent River. Because the ALQ-99 pods were not designed for subsonic flight, an aerodynamic redesign of the pod is being considered to accommodate the Super Hornet's flight profile. Given the aircraft's 11 hardpoints, it should be able to carry two ALQ-99 pods, two HARM missiles, and two air-to-air missiles for self-defense. Another possible configuration is five pods, although this will reduce overall range somewhat.

Recently, the Marine Corps has expressed interest in the program to replace its Prowlers.

The Analysis of Alternatives presently underway is a five-phase effort, the third phase of which was completed on 21 September 2000. An industry study of available technologies has also been completed which lays the foundation for future modeling and simulation work. Following approval of the efforts through phase three by the Executive Steering group, phase four analysis will commence with a written report (the culmination of phase five) due out 1 December 2001. Besides the F/A-18G, other options under consideration during the Analysis of Alternatives program are use of small UCAVs, an electronic warfare adaptation of the Boeing 757 and 767 airliners, and electronic warfare variants of the F-15, F-22 and JSF.

THE SUPER HORNET AS A TANKER

During the 1970s and '80s organic air wing tanking was supplied via the KA-6D Intruder. Other aircraft, such as the A-7E, A-6E, and S-3A/B, also provided tanking with buddy stores, but not as effectively as the KA-6D. Moreover, the A-7 was retired in 1992. The retirement of the

Intruders in 1996, however, left the carrier air wing completely dependent on the S-3B and ES-3A (also now retired) for tanking around the ship, and placed a greater emphasis on the use of Air Force and Marine Corps tanker assets. Today, much of the Viking's flight time is devoted to tanking other air wing aircraft, and hardly an S-3B mission is flown without a buddy store.

The F/A-18E equipped with up to four external 480-gallon tanks and a 330-gallon centerline A/A42R-1 aerial refueling store (ARS) (a total of 29,000 lbs. of fuel) brings the organic tanking asset back to the carrier. More importantly, because it flies the same profile as its stablemates, additional fuel economies are resultant. "The S-3 needs to launch a full 45 minutes early," one spokesperson said, "to be in a position for refueling if it is in an en route scenario. The E can get up, out, and established in the tanker circle much more quickly." A tanker configured F/A-18E can still carry air-to-air and

air-to-ground weapons needed for self-protection, which reduced the need for tanker escort. Even with tanks and the ARS, the F/A-18E/F can carry two AIM-9 Sidewinders, two AIM-120 AMRAAMs, and four AGM-88 HARMs.

According to Navy estimates comparing the current organic tanker, the S-3B, and an ARS-equipped F/A-18E, an S-3 on a "yo-yo" flight profile – flying up to 30 minutes to disperse fuel – can give 8,000 lbs. The F/A-18E, with two 480-gallon tanks and a 330-gallon centerline ARS, can give 12,000 lbs. of fuel. When configured as a mission tanker, the S-3 can provide 10,000 lbs.; the F/A-18E can offer 9,000 lbs. Since the Super Hornet is planned for a total of five "wet" stations, its superiority as an organic tanker is clear. Although tanks are currently cleared for only the two inboard and the centerline stations, the Navy plans to have all five cleared for the Super Hornet's first deployment with VFA-115.

The Super Hornet brings yet another mission to strike-fighters bag of goods. For the first time since the departure of the dedicated KA-6D Intruder, carrier air wings will have a capable organic tanking asset. The F/A-18E has an internal fuel capacity of 14,500 lbs., and is also plumbed to carry five 480-gallon external tanks, or four such tanks and a 330-gallon buddy pod for a total of 29,000 lbs. (Boeing)

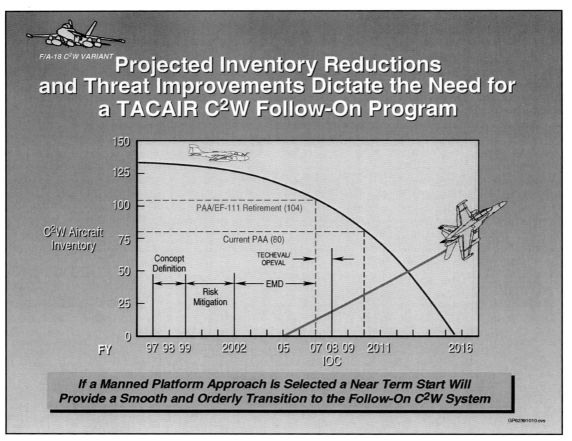

F/A-18 C²W VARIANT

Projected Inventory Reductions and Threat Improvements Dictate the Need for a TACAIR C²W Follow-On Program

C²W Aircraft Inventory

- 150
- 125
- 100 — PAA/EF-111 Retirement (104)
- 75 — Current PAA (80)
- 50
- 25
- 0

Concept Definition | Risk Mitigation | EMD | TECHEVAL/OPEVAL

FY 97 98 99 2002 05 07 08 09 2011 2016
IOC

If a Manned Platform Approach Is Selected a Near Term Start Will Provide a Smooth and Orderly Transition to the Follow-On C²W System

GP62391010.cvs

This Boeing chart shows the projected inventory reductions and threat improvements, and highlights the need for a Prowler follow-on. Operations over the Balkans have demonstrated that the EA-6B is invaluable in a high-threat air defense environment. (Boeing)

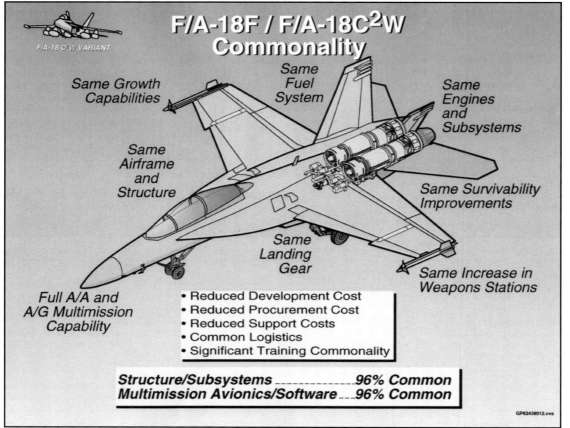

F/A-18 C²W VARIANT

F/A-18F / F/A-18C²W Commonality

- Same Growth Capabilities
- Same Fuel System
- Same Engines and Subsystems
- Same Airframe and Structure
- Same Survivability Improvements
- Same Landing Gear
- Same Increase in Weapons Stations
- Full A/A and A/G Multimission Capability

- Reduced Development Cost
- Reduced Procurement Cost
- Reduced Support Costs
- Common Logistics
- Significant Training Commonality

Structure/Subsystems _____ 96% Common
Multimission Avionics/Software _____ 96% Common

GP62438012.cvs

One advantage the C2W has over other vehicles being considered under the Analysis of Alternatives is its commonality of airframe with the F/A-18F. Structures and subsystems as well as multi-mission avionics and software are 96 percent common. The major changes come in added software to accommodate the electronic warfare missions. (Boeing)

HORNET OPERATORS

THE F/A-18 IN SQUADRON SERVICE

United States

United States Navy

— Atlantic Fleet —

Squadron	Name	Base	Est'd/Transitioned–To	Model
VFA-15	Valions	NAS Oceana, VA	1986 – Present	F/A-18C(N)
VFA-34	Blue Blasters	NAS Oceana, VA	1996 – Present	F/A-18C(N)
VFA-37	Bulls	NAS Oceana, VA	1991 – Present	F/A-18C(N)
VFA-81	Sunliners	NAS Oceana, VA	1988 – Present	F/A-18C
VFA-83	Rampagers	NAS Oceana, VA	1988 – Present	F/A-18C
VFA-87	Golden Warriors	NAS Oceana, VA	1986 – Present	F/A-18C(N)
VFA-105	Gunslingers	NAS Oceana, VA	1991 – Present	F/A-18C(N)
VFA-106*	Gladiators	NAS Oceana, VA	1984 – Present	F/A-18A/B/C/D
VFA-131	Wildcats	NAS Oceana, VA	1983 – Present	F/A-18C(N)
VFA-136	Knighthawks	NAS Oceana, VA	1985 – Present	F/A-18C(N)
VFA-82	Marauders	MCAS Beaufort, SC	1987 – Present	F/A-18C
VFA-86	Sidewinders	MCAS Beaufort, SC	1987 – Present	F/A-18C

— Pacific Fleet —

Squadron	Name	Base	Est'd/Transitioned–To	Model
VFA-22	Fighting Redcocks	NAS Lemoore, CA	1990 – Present	F/A-18C(N)
VFA-25	Fist of the Fleet	NAS Lemoore, CA	1983 – Present	F/A-18C(N)
VFA-94	Mighty Shrikes	NAS Lemoore, CA	1991 – Present	F/A-18C(N)
VFA-97	Warhawks	NAS Lemoore, CA	1991 – Present	F/A-18A
VFA-113	Stingers	NAS Lemoore, CA	1983 – Present	F/A-18C(N)
VFA-115	Eagles	NAS Lemoore, CA	1996 – Present	F/A-18C(N)
VFA-122*	Flying Eagles	NAS Lemoore, CA	1999 – Present	F/A-18E/F
VFA-125*	Rough Raiders	NAS Lemoore, CA	1981 – Present	F/A-18A/B/C/D
VFA-137	Kestrels	NAS Lemoore, CA	1985 – Present	F/A-18C(N)
VFA-146	Blue Diamonds	NAS Lemoore, CA	1989 – Present	F/A-18C(N)
VFA-147	Argonauts	NAS Lemoore, CA	1989 – Present	F/A-18C(N)
VFA-151	Vigilantes	NAS Lemoore, CA	1986 – Present	F/A-18C(N)
VFA-27	Royal Maces	NAF Atsugi, Japan	1991 – Present	F/A-18C(N)
VFA-192	Golden Dragons	NAF Atsugi, Japan	1985 – Present	F/A-18C
VFA-195	Dambusters	NAF Atsugi, Japan	1985 – Present	F/A-18C

* Fleet Replenishment Squadron (FRS)

U.S. Naval Reserve Squadrons

Squadron	Name	Base	Est'd/Transitioned–To	Model
VFA-203	Blue Dolphins	NAS Atlanta, GA	1989 – Present	F/A-18A
VFA-204	River Rattlers	JRB New Orleans, LA	1991 – Present	F/A-18A
VFA-303	Golden Hawks	NAS Lemoore, CA	1984 – 1994	F/A-18A
VFA-305	Lobos	NAS Point Mugu, VA	1987 – 1994	F/A-18A
VMFA-112	Cowboys	JRB Fort Worth, TX	1991 – Present	F/A-18A/B
VMFA-134	Smoke	MCAS Miramar, CA	1989 – Present	F/A-18A
VMFA-142	Flying Gators	NAS Atlanta, GA	1990 – Present	F/A-18A
VMFA-321	Hell's Angels	Andrews AFB, MD	1991 – Present	F/A-18A/B

United States Marine Corps

Squadron	Name	Base	Est'd/Transitioned–To	Model
VMFAT-101*	Sharpshooters	MCAS Miramar, CA	1987 – Present	F/A-18A/B/C/D
VMFA-115	Silver Eagles	MCAS Beaufort, SC	1985 – Present	F/A-18A
VMFA(AW)-121	Green Knights	MCAS Miramar, CA	1989 – Present	F/A-18D(N)
VMFA-122	Crusaders	MCAS Beaufort, SC	1986 – Present	F/A-18A
VMFA-212	Lancers	MCAS Miramar, CA	1988 – Present	F/A-18C
VMFA(AW)-224	Bengals	MCAS Beaufort, SC	1991 – Present	F/A-18D(N)
VMFA(AW)-225	Vikings	MCAS Miramar, CA	1991 – Present	F/A-18D(N)
VMFA-232	Red Devils	MCAS Miramar, CA	1989 – Present	F/A-18C
VMFA(AW)-242	Bats	MCAS Miramar, CA	1991 – Present	F/A-18D(N)
VMFA-251	Thunderbolts	MCAS Beaufort, SC	1986 – Present	F/A-18C(N)
VMFA-312	Checkerboards	MCAS Beaufort, SC	1988 – Present	F/A-18C(N)
VMFA-314	Black Knights	MCAS Miramar, CA	1982 – Present	F/A-18C(N)
VMFA-323	Death Rattlers	MCAS Miramar, CA	1982 – Present	F/A-18C(N)
VMFA(AW)-332	Moonlighters	MCAS Beaufort, SC	1993 – Present	F/A-18D(N)
VMFA(AW)-533	Hawks	MCAS Beaufort, SC	1991 – Present	F/A-18D(N)

Disestablished U.S. Squadrons

Squadron	Name	Base	Est'd/Transitioned–To	Model
VF-45	Blackbirds	NAS Key West, FL	1987 – 1996	F/A-18A
VFA-127	Desert Bogies	NAS Fallon, NV	1992 – 1996	F/A-18A/B
VFA-132	Privateers	NAS Cecil Field, FL	1984 – 1992	F/A-18A
VFA-161	Chargers	NAS Lemoore, CA	1986 – 1988	F/A-18A
VMFA-235	Death Angels	MCAS Miramar, CA	1989 – 1996	F/A-18C
VMFA-333	Shamrocks	MCAS Beaufort, SC	1987 – 1992	F/A-18A
VMFA-451	Warlords	MCAS Beaufort, SC	1987 – 1997	F/A-18A
VMFA-531	Grey Ghosts	MCAS El Toro, CA	1983 – 1992	F/A-18A

*Fleet Replenishment Squadron (FRS)

U.S. Navy Special Squadrons

Squadron	Name	Base	Est'd/Transitioned–To	Model
VAQ-34	Electric Horsemen	NAS Lemoore, CA	1990 – 1993	F/A-18A/B
VFC–12	Fighting Omars	NAS Oceana, VA	1988 – Present	F/A-18A/B
VFC-13	Saints	NAS Fallon, NV	1988 – 1996	F/A-18A/B
VX-4[1]	Evaluators	NAS Point Mugu, CA	1980 – 1994	F/A-18A/C/D
VX-5[1]	Vampires	NAWS China Lake, CA	1982 – 1994	F/A-18A/B/C/D
VX-9	Evaluators	NAWS China Lake, CA	1994 – Present	F/A-18C/D/E/F
NAWC-WD	Dust Devils	NAWS China Lake, CA	1983 – Present	F/A-18C/D/E/F
NFDS	Blue Angels	NAS Pensacola, FL	1987 – Present	F/A–18A/B
NFWS	Top Gun	NAS Miramar, CA	1987 – 1996	F/A-18A/B
NSATS	Salty Dog	NAS Patuxent River, MD	1983 – 1996	F/A-18C/D/E/F
NSAWC		NAS Fallon, NV	1996 – Present	F/A-18A/B
NSWC	Strike U	NAS Fallon, NV	1986 – 1996	F/A-18A/B
NWEF		Kirtland AFB. NM		F/A-18A
USNTPS	Tea Kettle	NAS Patuxent River, MD	1986 – Present	F/A-18B/D

*Merged into VX-9 in 1994.

International Operators

Royal Australian Air Force

Squadron	Name	Base	Est'd/Transitioned– To	Model
No. 2 OCU		RAAF Williamtown	1985 – Present	AF-18A/B
No. 3 Sqn		RAAF Williamtown	1986 – Present	AF-18A/B
No. 75 Sqn		RAAF Tindal	1988 – Present	AF-18A/B
No. 77 Sqn		RAAF Williamtown	1987 – Present	AF-18A/B
ARDU		RAAF Edinburgh	1985 – Present	AF-18A/B

Canadian Forces

Squadron	Name	Base	Est'd/Transitioned– To	Model
No. 409 Sqn	Nighthawks	Baden-Soellingen	1984 – 1991	CF-18A/B
No. 410 TF(TO)S	Cougars	CFB Cold Lake	1982 – Present	CF-18A/B
No. 416 Sqn	Lynxes	CFB Cold Lake	1988 – Present	CF-18A/B
No. 421 Sqn	Red Indians	Baden-Soellingen	1986 – 1992	CF-18A/B
No. 425 Sqn	Alouettes	CFB Bagotville	1985 – Present	CF-18A/B
No. 433 Sqn	Porcupines	CFB Bagotville	1987 – Present	CF-18A/B
No. 439 Sqn	Tigers	Baden-Soellingen	1987 – 1992	CF-18A/B
No. 441 Sqn	Silver Foxes	CFB Cold Lake	1985 – Present	CF-18A/B
AETE		CFB Cold Lake	1982 – Present	CF-18A/B

Llmavoimat (Finnish Air Force)

Squadron	Name	Base	Est'd/Transitioned– To	Model
HävLLv 11	Lapin Wing	Rovaniemi	1998 – Present	F-18C/D
HävLLv 21	Satakunnan Wing	Tampere-Pirkkala	1995 – Present	F-18C/D
HävLLv 31	Karjalan Wing	Kuopio-Rissala	1996 – Present	F-18C/D
Koelentokeskus		Halli	1997 – Present	F-18C/D

Al Quwwat al Jawwiya al Kuwaitiya (Kuwait Air Force)

Squadron	Name	Base	Est'd/Transitioned–To	Model
No. 9 Sqn		Ahemd al Jaber AB	1993 – Present	F/A-18C/D
No. 25 Sqn		Ali al Salem AB	1992 – Present	F/A-18C/D

Tentara Udara Diraja Malaysia (Royal Malasian Air Force)

Squadron	Name	Base	Est'd/Transitioned–To	Model
18 Night Figher Skuadron		Butterworth	1997 – Present	F/A-18D

Eército del Aire Español (Spanish Air Force)

Squadron	Name	Base	Est'd/Transitioned–To	Model
Escuadron 121		Torrejon de Ardoz	1986 – Present	EF-18A/B+
Escuadron 122		Torrejon de Ardoz	1987 – Present	EF-18A/B+
Escuadron 124		Torrejon de Ardoz	1992 – 1994	EF-18A/B+
Escuadron 151		Zaragoza-Valenzuela	1989 – Present	EF-18A/B+
Escuadron 152		Zaragoza-Valenzuela	1989 – Present	EF-18A/B+
Escuadron 153		Zaragoza-Valenzuela	1995 – Present	EF-18B+
Escuadron 211		Morón	1996 – Present	EF-18A/B+
CLAEX		Torrejón	1987 – Present	EF-18A+

Schweizerische Flugwaffe/Troupe d'Aviation Suisse (Swiss Air Force)

Squadron	Name	Base	Est'd/Transitioned–To	Model
Fliegerstaffel 11		Meiringen	1999 – Present	F-18C/D
Fliegerstaffel 17		Payerne	1997 – Present	F-18C/D
Fliegerstaffel 18		Sion	1998 – Present	F-18C/D

SIGNIFICANT DATES

1965
Northrop begins work on N-300 multi-role fighter.

26 January 1971
Northrop unveils P-530 design.

13 January 1972
Contacts awarded to General Dynamics and Northrop to develop YF-16 and YF-17.

4 April 1974
First YF-17 rolls out at Hawthorn facility.

9 June 1974
First YF-17 makes maiden flight.

2 May 1975
Navy given go-ahead to develop a navalized derivative of YF-17.

22 January 1976
Contract award to McDonnell Douglas to develop F-18.

18 November 1978
First FSD F-18 makes maiden flight.

1 April 1984
DoD officially redesignates F-18 as F/A-18.

15 July 1987
DoD orders McDonnell Douglas to develop derivative of F/A-18.

7 January 1991
A-12 Program canceled.

12 May 1992
Navy announces F/A-18E/F program.

13-17 June 1994
F/A-18E/F critical design review.

May 1995
F/A-18E1 final assembly begins at McDonnell Douglas.

General Electric delivers the first production F414 engines.

19 September 1995
F/A-18E1 roll-out ceremony, ADM Jeremy Boorda, Chief of Naval Operations, names the E/F the Super Hornet.

29 November 1995
E1's first flight took place in St. Louis, Missouri.

14 February 1996
F/A-18E2 arrives at Patuxent River, Maryland.

March 1996
Program receives the first U.S. Department of Defense Acquisition Excellence Award.

April 1996
Program gets the go-ahead to procure low-rate initial production of long-lead parts.

McDonnell Douglas and Northrop Grumman team to develop a plan to have an electronic warfare variant of the two-seat F/A-18F achieve initial operational capacity between 2007 and 2009.

1 April 1996
F1's first flight took place in St. Louis.

12-13 April 1996
F/A-18E1 completes the first supersonic test flights for the E/F flight test program. The aircraft achieves a speed of Mach 1.1 on 12 April and Mach 1.52 on 13 April.

14 May 1996
Program surpasses 100 flight hours.

21 May 1996
McDonnell Douglas delivers the first two-seat F/A-18E/F Super Hornet (F1) to Patuxent River.

22 May 1996
F/A-18E2 completes the longest single flight (five hours) to date for the E/F flight test program.

13 June 1996
Test program surpasses 100 flights.

July 1996
F/A-18E/F Integrated Test Team named winner of The Order of the Daedalians Weapon System Award for 1995, honoring those who have made major contributions to the development of an outstanding weapon system.

2 July 1996
E4's first flight took place in St. Louis.

5 August 1996
F/A-18F1 performs first steam ingestion catapults at Pax River.

October 1996
Program wins Aircraft Design Award from the American Institute of Aeronautics and Astronautics.

29 October 1996
Program surpasses 500 flight hours.

1997
QDR slashes E/F procurement from 1,000 to 548 and raises JSF.

January 1997
F1 successfully completes initial sea trials aboard USS *John C. Stennis* one week earlier than scheduled.

22 January 1997
F/A-18F2 arrives at Pax River.

1 February 1997
F/A-18E3 arrives at Patuxent River, marking the arrival of the seventh and final E/F flight test aircraft.

19 February 1997
F/A-18E/Fs successfully completes the test program's first stores separation test by dropping an empty 480-gallon fuel tank from 5,000 feet.

26 February 1997
F/A-18E/Fs makes first flight with three 480-gallon tanks separated from centerline and wing stations.

27 March 1997
LRIP approved.

5 April 1997
F/A-18F2 fired the first missile of the flight test program — an AIM-9.

May 1997
Center/aft assembly entered production at Northrop Grumman.

1 May 1997
Successfully completed drop test program.

August 1997
Super Hornet begins barricade engagement testing.

4 August 1997
Boeing and McDonnell Douglas merge.

29 August 1997
1,500th flight-hour by F/A-18E1.

12 September 1997
1,000th test flight flown by Super Hornet F/A-18E4.

15 September 1997
Super Hornet enters production at The Boeing Company.

13 November 1997
Clean aircraft new technologies demonstration completed.

20 November 1997
First operational test completed.

5 December 1997
AIM-9 wingtip and AIM-120 fuselage launches completed.

8 December 1997
2,000 flight-hour, flown by F2.

25 February 1998
F1 ferried to Lakehurst, New Jersey for carrier suitability tests.

23 March 1998
F1 completes suitability tests.

March 1998
LRIP II production funding approved.

LRIP III advanced procurement funding approved.

April 1998
F/A-18F2 transitions to China Lake.

19 June 1998
First production Super Hornet fuselage (E6) joined.

August 1998
TO-IIB completed.

13 August 1998
General Electric delivered first F414 production engine.

23 October 1998
E1 completes EMD flutter program one month ahead of schedule.

6 November 1998
E6 completes successful first flight.

9 November 1998
Flight test program completes the 2,500 flight.

February 1999
Second series of carrier quals on USS *Harry S. Truman.*

27 May 1999
OpEval begins with VX-9.

November 1999
OpEval ends.

November 1999
VFA-122 receives its first production E/F.

June 2000
VFA-122 commences training of E/F crews.

25 August 2000
Last F/A-18C/D delivered.

14 September 2000
Hornets reach 4,000,000th flight hour.

2002
First expected Super Hornet deployment by VFA-115 aboard USS *Abraham Lincoln.*